WAITING WELL

Maximizing the Journey of Singleness

By
Kayla Fointno

Waiting Well:
Maximizing the Journey of Singleness

By: Kayla Fointno

BOOKS BY KJF
Self-Publishing
"Everyone has a book on the inside of them waiting to be discovered."

Waiting Well: Maximizing the Journey of Singleness
Copyright © 2022 by Kayla Fointno
All rights reserved.

Scanning, uploading, and distribution of this book without permission is a theft of the author's intellectual property. No part of this publication may be reproduced, stored in a retrieval system, or transmitted in any form or by any means-electronic, mechanical, photocopy, recording, or any other-except for brief quotations in printed reviews, without the prior permission of the published.

Published By: Books By KJF Self-Publishing, LLC
ISBN: 978-1-7358846-8-4 (Hardback)
ISBN: 978-1-7358846-7-7 (Paperback)
ISBN: 978-1-7358846-9-1 (EBook)
Library of Congress Control Number: 2022922420

Contributors:

Editor: Darian Nealy
Cover Photograph by James Wayne

Scripture quotations marked (NLT) are taken from the *Holy Bible*, New Living Translation, copyright ©1996, 2004, 2015 by Tyndale House Foundation. Used by permission of Tyndale House Publishers, Carol Stream, Illinois 60188. All rights reserved.

Scripture quotations marked MSG are taken from THE MESSAGE, copyright © 1993, 2002, 2018 by Eugene H. Peterson. Used by permission of NavPress. All rights reserved. Represented by Tyndale House Publishers, Inc.

THE HOLY BIBLE, NEW INTERNATIONAL VERSION®, NIV® Copyright © 1973, 1978, 1984, 2011 by Biblica, Inc.® Used by permission. All rights reserved worldwide.

Scripture quotations marked HCSB are taken from the Holman Christian Standard Bible®, Copyright © 1999, 2000, 2002, 2003, 2009 by Holman Bible Publishers. Used by permission. Holman Christian Standard Bible®, Holman CSB®, and HCSB® are federally registered trademarks of Holman Bible Publishers.

Scripture taken from the New King James Version®. Copyright © 1982 by Thomas Nelson. Used by permission. All rights reserved.

Also used: King James Version which is public domain.

Also used: American Standard Version which is public domain.

Dedication:

To my God, my friend, my first love: I could recite the password to our secret place (Psalms 100:4 (MSG)) a billion times and that would never be enough. So, I vow to show you thanks with the way I live my life.

To the one whom my soul already loves: I don't know you, yet I already love you. I don't know you, yet I thank God every time I think of you walking this Earth. Your heartbeat is subconsciously my favorite hymn and the cadence of my steps. I thank every life experience you've had because it will lead you right to me. God has anointed me to be your bride and you to be my bridegroom. He has been pre-*pairing* us for this union all our lives. I am confident you and I already dwell under the same star and my heart is full knowing one day soon we will dwell together.

To my season of singlehood: Thank you for the tears. Thank you for the love. Thank you for the growth, the knowledge and wisdom. Thank you for the contentment. Thank you for the journey. Thank you for pushing me closer to the Father. Even when we part ways, the time we have spent together will always hold a special place in my heart. Upon the ending of our season together, may I never see you again.

Love, Kayla

EPIGRAPH:

"But rather seek ye the kingdom of God; and all these things shall be added unto you."

        Luke 12:31 (KJV)

Contents

SECTION 1: INTRODUCTION 1
    CHAPTER ONE: Singleness 2

SECTION 2: SELF-AWARENESS ASSESSMENT 8
    CHAPTER TWO: What Phase of Singleness Are You In? 9

SECTION 3: WORKING AND WAITING 19
    CHAPTER THREE: Purpose 20
    CHAPTER FOUR: Know Yourself, Know Your Worth 32
    CHAPTER FIVE: Vision 42

SECTION 4: THE JOURNEY OF MAXIMIZATION 53
    CHAPTER SIX: A Spouse Cannot Be Earned. They Are A Gift, Not A Reward. 54
    CHAPTER SEVEN: Be Careful Not To Awaken Love Before It's Time 61
    CHAPTER EIGHT: Why Sexual Purity? 70

SECTION 5: ARE YOU WILLING? 105
    CHAPTER NINE: Are You Committed to The Pour? 106
    CHAPTER TEN: Release It (Soul Detox) 114

SECTION 6: GET READY. GET SET. MAXIMIZE! 127
    CHAPTER ELEVEN: Go Forth and Maximize 128

SECTION 7: BONUS 133
    CHAPTER 12: I Didn't Maximize My Singleness and Now I'm In A Relationship 134

About The Author 140

SECTION 1

INTRODUCTION

CHAPTER ONE

Singleness

Singleness is, unapologetically and without consideration, taking the last piece of cake. Singleness is having all the closet space to yourself. It's spending your Saturday doing what makes *you* happy and not having to think about another person. Unfortunately, singleness is also answering the never-ending questions, "Have you found someone yet?" with a side of, "You're great; how are you still single?" and a fan favorite, "You're just too picky." If it weren't for these questions and a few others about your current relationship status, maybe singleness wouldn't be so bad, but alas, we live in a fallen world where people don't think before they speak.

Oftentimes this world idolizes marriage and the idea of marriage, but neglects that same energy towards singleness. This in turn makes singles feel as if there's something wrong with them or even pressures them into relationships just to achieve the status of "taken." From random children at the grocery store to the IRS, everyone wants to know your current status—it's exhausting, really. As if these statuses will be the barometer of which God judges us come that fateful day or as if these statuses are going to get us into the VIP section of Heaven. Onlookers to our singleness fail to realize that to be single and to be married are both a gift from God; Paul reminds us of that in 1 Corinthians 7:7 (MSG), "Sometimes I wish everyone were single like me—a simpler life in many ways! But celibacy is not for everyone any more than marriage is. God gives the gift of the single life to some, the gift of the married life to others." Both these seasons in life are important, with singleness possibly being the most important. Singleness is the time with God where He is the one who monopolizes your time with no interruptions. Paul goes on to explain it like this in 1 Corinthians 7:32-35 (NIV), "I would like you to be free from concern. An unmarried man is concerned about the Lord's affairs—how he can please the Lord. But a married man is concerned about the affairs of this world—how he can please his wife— and his interests are divided. An unmarried woman or virgin is concerned about the Lord's affairs: Her aim is to be devoted to the Lord in both body and spirit. But a married woman is concerned about the affairs of this world—how she can please her husband. I am saying this for your own good, not to restrict you, but that you may live in a right way in undivided devotion to the Lord." A single person's time and interest shouldn't be divided; they should solely be focused on God...in a perfect world. Because let's be honest, your time and interest are on God, but also on the dating app or wherever else you could possibly meet your future spouse. If a single person's heart *was* solely focused on God, it wouldn't be so much unfulfillment during the season of singleness. This season was never meant to rise and fall at the meeting of another person who needs a savior just like you. Your singleness is about spending the most time with God possible; it is about serving His kingdom with no reservation. It's not about looking for "the one" and daydreaming about how God will finally bless you. That is idol worship and God will never give you a gift that will compete with Him. He would rather see you single than in a relationship where a mere human being is on the throne of your heart, as an idol in your life.

A final aspect of singleness that needs to be highlighted:

Before the season of hibernation, most animals have the mindset to plan ahead. They know what is to come in the next season, so they do all they can to prepare themselves and their family for a long season of hibernation. They store and hoard in preparation so when the season comes, they are lacking nothing. While this is great, I believe we as singles, people really, have taken this and twisted it; neglecting to find a balance. We plan ahead and prepare ourselves, but we also hoard life as if Moses didn't ask God to, "teach us to number our days…" (Psalms 90:12). We wait to go there, try that, or be here. Storing up life's experiences is seemingly done with good intentions, but this is not God's desire for us. Hoarding these experiences on our to-do list so they can be enjoyed with a significant other is deficit living. In fact, it's quite presumptuous to live life on pause with the expectation that one day our significant other will come, and we can finally press play on life's experiences. Since tomorrow is not promised to anyone, why treat each day like a countdown and every new year alone like doomsday? If for one second you could get an aerial perspective and see what God sees, you would know this is not what God intended for your life. God intended for you to enjoy the abundant life (John 10:10). Whether you file your taxes as single or as married—your *one* life should be lived with no regrets.

So, I ask you, how well are you waiting during your season of singleness? Are you putting off life experiences or are you living life to the fullest? Have you done the heart work, or have you let your heart work you (Jeremiah 17:9)? Do you know your purpose? Do you *really* know yourself? Do you have a vision for your life? Have you even begun to heal?

I know, *deep breaths…in through your nose and out through your mouth* (repeat as needed)

Once you've reached a place of serenity, take some time to evaluate your singleness thus far. Whether it's been interrupted by "Could've Beens" or filled with continuity. Document the progression or even regression you've made and what you've learned along your journey thus far:

Singleness

Waiting Well

SECTION 2

SELF - AWARENESS ASSESSMENT

CHAPTER TWO

What Phase of Singleness Are You In?

Self-awareness is an important feature for a single person, it separates you from being haphazardly single and being single with purpose; however, this type of introspection is not for the weak.

Check And/Or Highlight All That Apply:

❏ **Where art thou (@future boo)?**

   1 Samuel 13: 8-14 (NIV)

   "He waited seven days, the time set by Samuel; but Samuel did not come to Gilgal, and Saul's men began to scatter. So he said, "Bring me the burnt offering and the *fellowship offerings." And Saul offered up the burnt offering. Just as he finished making the offering, Samuel arrived, and Saul went out to greet him. "What have you done?" asked Samuel. Saul replied, "When I saw that the men were scattering, and that you did not come at the set time, and that the Philistines were assembling at Mikmash, I thought, 'Now the Philistines will come down against me at Gilgal, and I have not sought the Lord's favor.' So I felt compelled to offer the burnt offering." "You have done a foolish thing," Samuel said. "You have not kept the command the Lord your God gave you; if you had, he would have established your kingdom over Israel for all time. But now your kingdom will not endure; the Lord has sought out a man after his own heart and appointed him ruler of his people, because you have not kept the Lord's command."*

❖ "I realize I've been trying to do God's job and play matchmaker myself because I didn't want to wait for God's perfect timing."

❖ "Just like Saul, the pressures from my surroundings and my circumstance made me sacrifice pieces of my legacy."

❖ "If I'm being honest, I never got God's green light confirmation for anyone I've dated."

❏ **I'm going to be alone forever.**

> Genesis 2:18 (NKJV)
>
> "And the Lord God said, "It is not good that man should be alone; I will make him a helper comparable to him.""

❖ "Swiping left and right, sliding in and out of dm's obviously isn't working well for me."

❖ "If I go on one more first date I will scream!"

❖ "I feel like I've searched the ends of the Earth looking for a mate; *maybe I'll try Mars.*"

❖ "God was the one that said it wasn't good for man to be alone, but I guess I'm the exception to policy."

> 2 Corinthians 6:14 (NIV)
>
> "Do not be yoked together with unbelievers. For what do righteousness and wickedness have in common? Or what fellowship can light have with darkness?"

❖ "I'm one dating app away from going back to my toxic ex."

❖ "What ever happened to that cute person I went to high school with? Maybe I should reach out?"

❖ "If we start dating, I can change them and they'll love God like I do in no time!"

- ❏ **God has someone for me, so I'm currently waiting patiently.**

    Psalms 27:14 (NLT)

    "Wait patiently for the Lord. Be brave and courageous. Yes, wait patiently for the Lord."

- ❖ "God has someone for me, so I'm going to stop doing His job. I will now wait patiently and with purpose!"

- ❖ "I'm waiting with expectancy. I don't know when, but I know God will send that person when the time is right."

- ❖ "Waiting is hard. Some days I'm okay with being single, some days I'm not. Through it all, God is purposeful, faithful, and omnipresent."

    Matthew 6:33 (ASV)

    "But seek ye first his kingdom, and his righteousness; and all these things shall be added unto you."

- ❖ "I'm trusting the process. In the meantime, I'll serve the Lord while my time is not divided between God and man."

- ❖ "Growing in my walk with God. I'm falling in love with Him and myself."

❖ "It's almost like I have more clarity ever since I stopped focusing on when my future spouse would come. A weight has been lifted off my shoulders and scales dropped from my eyes. I can finally see what God wants to do in this season."

❑ **Been there, disappointed, so I'm just doing me.**

Job 13:15 (KJV)

"Though he slay me, yet will I trust in him: but I will maintain mine own ways before him."

❖ "That last relationship tried to break me. I can never love again."

❖ "I don't expect anything from a God that would allow me to go through so much pain. I have neither faith nor expectation."

❖ "I'm going to become cold and heartless; I don't care who I hurt in the process. I'll never be that vulnerable with anyone again."

❖ "I'm F-R-E-E...you know the rest. *sighs* Maybe I'll join a convent."

Waiting Well

Proverbs 3:5 (KJV)

"Trust in the Lord with all thine heart and lean not unto thine own understanding."

❖ "Why would God allow me to go through this much pain?"

❖ "I was with someone who I thought was my Boaz/Ruth; I don't understand why it ended."

❖ "I'm completely over it, but I still want to know what I did wrong? What could I have done to keep the relationship? Why did God take away the only person I have ever loved?"

❏ **Alexa, play "I'm living my best life."**

Psalms 30:11 (NLT)

"You have turned my mourning into joyful dancing. You have taken away my clothes of mourning and clothed me with joy."

❖ "I was in a bad place after that relationship, but thank God I've got my faith back."

❖ "I was upset with God because of my past experiences, but Faith+ Expectation= Miracle."

> Psalms 37:4 (NKJV)
>
> "Delight yourself also in the Lord, And He shall give you the desires of your heart."

- ❖ "I'm serving looks and Jesus. The joy of my salvation is glowing in the warm sun. God is laying a firm foundation of faith in my life. I'm living my life and season's purpose. I'm in my zone! I'm doing well! I-N-D-E-P-E-N-D-E-N-T, because I've got joy, joy, joy....in my soul!"

- ❖ "I never thought I would get to a place where God would be enough for me, but He is. I am content in my singleness. (But God don't get any ideas because I don't want to be single longer than I need to be, amen!)"

- ❖ "Even if someone were to come into my life right now, they will always be playing for second, because Jesus has captured my heart."

❏ **Season of Preparation.**

> Ezekiel 38:7 (NKJV)
>
> "Prepare yourself and be ready, you and all your companies that are gathered about you; and be a guard for them."

- "I'm making space for the person God has for me to come into my life."
- "I'm maximizing my singleness."
- "I'm gaining insight and wisdom in the area of Kingdom Relationships/Marriages."
- "God is revealing to me the areas I need to work on before I enter into another relationship."

- ❏ **He who finds a wife.. "I'm waiting to be found. I'm looking for the one, have you seen her?"**

    Proverbs 18:22 (KJV)

    "Whoso findeth a wife findeth a good thing, And obtaineth favour of the LORD."

- "I'm waiting for my favor, my good thing, but I know God is in control."
- "The Lord says I'm a "good thing" so I'm waiting to be found, but I know God is in control."

    Isaiah 40:31 (KJV)

    "but they that wait upon the LORD shall renew their strength; they shall mount up with wings as eagles; they shall run, and not be weary; and they shall walk, and not faint."

- "It could happen any day now, I just hope I look good when it does!"

- "They say it comes when you least expect it, so I'm going to keep serving God and walking in my purpose. When this person comes, we'll serve God and walk in purpose together."

❏ **In transition.**

Philippians 4:6 (NIV)

"Do not be anxious about anything, but in every situation, by prayer and petition, with thanksgiving, present your requests to God."

- "I met someone."
- "I really, really, really like them."
- "The Bible says to test the spirits to see if they're from God (1 John 4:1). Even though I really like this person I want to remain sober in mind so I can ensure this is not a devil in a blue suit/dress, aka, a counterfeit."

Matthew 17:21 (HCSB)

"However, this kind does not come out except by prayer and fasting."

- ❖ "I feel like I'm already falling in love, so before I get too love drunk, I'm going to pray and fast to see if this person should really be in my life. If they are to be in my life, I need to know how God wants me to steward over this relationship."

- ❖ "I've fasted, I've prayed. God has given me direction for this relationship. I'm not saying they're the one just yet, but this is something special God has sent me."

Meditate and reflect on the box(es) you have checked and the status you've highlighted. Maybe even date it to capture the exact time in history you felt this way. As the seasons change, so will your mindset. Be sure to update your checked box(es) with a date should your feelings change and use it as a point of reference to reflect.

SECTION 3

WORKING AND WAITING

CHAPTER THREE

Purpose

Pray, Worship, and Serve the Kingdom of God.

What does purpose mean to you?

_____

_____

_____

_____

_____

Purpose

Contrary to popular belief, purpose is not a final destination, nor definitive. Purpose is ever-evolving just like you and me. There is not an ultimate goal or finish line for our purpose in life; if there were, we would be God. If there were, once we have achieved the pinnacle of success, we would be perfect—growth no longer necessary. You and I both know that couldn't be further from the truth.

Unfortunately, we have been conditioned for so long to think purpose was a destination and to put our value in a job, a person, a thing, or what we can contribute to society. We have been conditioned to see purpose as this golden ticket on a hill to work towards. Nothing else matters until we've reached that ticket. God is not a destination type of God. He loves taking His kids on a journey. Why do you think He took the Children of Israel the scenic route? (See Exodus 13:17-18). So many go unfulfilled and believe they're wasting their life because society has force-fed them thoughts of inadequacy. Thinking there is no "purpose" in the off-seasons, feeling as if they are aimlessly wandering throughout life, and conveniently forgetting that our God says He will use *all* things (Romans 8:28). God uses the off seasons, the on seasons and everything in-between.

To combat the world's way of thinking, there are two somewhat rhetorical questions that need to be aired:

Question #1: If purpose is God's reasoning or His objective for your life, why would you be content with it *just* being a destination?

Question #2: Why would you choose to make your bed in complacency, allowing God to simply take you to that *one* place of intention for your life, then disappearing out of the details?

It's important to understand that purpose is seasonal because God works in and out of time. This is not to be confused with our very own winter, summer, spring, and fall; your season could be three months, but it could also be three years. The point is, your purpose is God-given steps of obedience, conquered at every turn, only to lead you to the next conquest or assignment. Each season's purpose, building off the next, taking you from glory to glory. God, using your current season's purpose as a vehicle to the next season's purpose and leading you one step at a time through *your* journey called life. As you live and breathe, you are in purpose, and you are purpose. Every day you wake up and have the opportunity to give God your obedience. As long as you have God's breath in your body, steadfast in His will, and obedient to His voice, you can never stop pursuing purpose because it never stops pursuing you. I challenge you: ask God for a fresh perspective. He will show you that just because you are not where you desire to be, doesn't mean He's not using your current season and your current situation. Quite the opposite—God is using your current situation to birth something in you for the next. How could you call a preparation season like that purposeless? God has been so gracious to intricately interconnect every season of your life. He knew you lining up your teddy bears as a child and "teaching" them, would be directly connected to you serving in the children's ministry. He knew that this would one day directly connect to you being a teacher in a classroom, and that would one day prepare you to build schools in foreign nations for the Kingdom of God. Every season of your life is purpose-filled when you're in the will of God. But I understand, you need some time to recover from the way of thinking that's been embedded in you since you were a child. Purpose being a final destination: You'd receive purpose by 30 and retire by 50. That way of thinking made you feel safe, in control. It made you feel like once you swiped the golden ticket of purpose you'd never have to wonder again or even be in a season of uncertainty, obscurity some might even say, but again, from Biblical evidence we've seen that's *not* how God operates. We're given the opportunity to discover God for the rest of our lives, so why shouldn't we have to discover ourselves as well? Our lives are not meant for autopilot, nor are they linear. They are full of twists, turns and inevitably, circles. The overall purpose of our lives is meant to be given in pieces. If God were to show you ALL the plans for your life right now, you would be overcome with pressure and self-sabotage. I know this for a fact because I would do the same. That's why purpose must be seasonal, "For we only know in part…" (1 Corinthians 13:9).

It is worthy of noting that while God gives us seasonal purposes, as believers there is an overarching purpose embedded in each season's purpose. That is to *Pray, Worship, and Serve the Kingdom of God* by carrying out the Great Commission for all that will believe (Matthew 28:18-20). As humans, we get so consumed with working unto man and what we want for ourselves that we forget our lives are not our own. Nowhere in the Bible does God say He wants us to be happy in the place and purpose of our choosing. God sends us where He needs a vessel and our mission is to *Pray, Worship, and Serve the Kingdom of God*, by carrying out the

Great Commission (Matthew 28:18-20) for all that will believe. In addition to this overarching purpose, because He is such a good God, He gives us joy and contentment in what we have to do and where He sends us.

God is the master of differentiation. Name a literary device, and He has used it at one point or another. That's what a good teacher does; they understand that all of their students don't learn the same and they adjust. God knows some need parables, some need to be shown, some need proximal examples, while others simply need to be told once. I'm going to take a page from God's book and provide a couple examples of how purpose can look:

Let's take King David, a shepherd boy, anointed for greatness by Samuel in front of his whole family. What did he do after Samuel anointed him? He went back into the fields with the sheep, until he was called to the Kingdom by Saul. (See 1 Samuel Chapter 16). David's future smelled like greatness—greatness for battle, for riches, for royalty; however, before God could take David to his next season of purpose (the Kingdom), God made sure David was cultivating his skills by taking him through a season of obedience. Had David not utilized the season before he was called, fighting bears and killing lions, he would have never had the wherewithal to defeat Goliath. In doing this, David honored God with his life by serving the Kingdom of God until his current situation became a vehicle to his next. David didn't sit and complain after he was anointed, wondering when God would use him. He made himself useful in his own realm of influence. He helped to build his family's empire by herding sheep and protecting them. He ministered to those around him, letting them see how God was moving in his life. All while praying, worshiping, and serving the Kingdom of God in the way that was requested of *him*.

Next, let's look at Peter. Peter's life had humble beginnings as a fisherman's son, learning the ropes of the family business. Peter knew his purpose from birth and probably imagined nothing beyond that. He settled on this path and figured he would ride this wave until death, that is until he met Jesus (that's worth shouting right there, but I digress). Imagine if he would have been disobedient to the calling on his life to become a fisherman? What if Peter would have taken his family and decided he didn't want to be a fisherman or live in Capernaum? What if he stepped out of God's will for his life, let his cousin have the family business and fled as far away from the Sea of Galilee as he could? Would he have been seen by Jesus? Peter's obedience to God in one season taught him the art of fishing and was directly attached to his next season—the art of fishing for men

(Matthew 4:19). As mundane as his days must have been doing the same thing repeatedly, God was preparing something in him. Had he been disobedient to this season of learning what it meant to be a fisherman, he would have never had the skills, nor the faith for the next season.

You might feel like God has placed you somewhere and forgotten you were there, but trust that wherever God has you is only a vehicle to the place He *will* show you (Genesis 12:1). There could be several reasons as to why you haven't yet been transported. One possibility worth highlighting is that maybe because you are neglecting the overarching purpose of believers—*Pray, Worship, and Serve the Kingdom of God*. Can the people you are currently surrounded by see Christ through you? Are you personifying an ambassador for the Kingdom of God or are you so worried about your future, that you have yet to find the contentment of Jesus Christ in your present? Another reason might be because of your lack of obedience. What is the last thing God told you to do? *That* is your purpose in this season; however, in disobedience, you will find yourself not only out of the Will of God, but *you* will be the reason you have not progressed to your next season of purpose. Yet and still, God is so gracious that even when you are disobedient, you are still *in* purpose. Your purpose may be cyclical, but it's a cycle you will inevitably learn from one day to advance you. Remember what the word of God says in Romans chapter 8 verse 28: "All things work together…" God is using every season, every job, every experience, every tear, every doubt, every frustration, every choice, and every repeated cycle to propel you into your next season of purpose. Nothing will be wasted in His Kingdom. I encourage you, sit in your season of purpose until it becomes a vehicle to your next. While you wait well, make certain you are doing the thing God has empowered us all to do, *Pray, worship, and serve the Kingdom of God.* (See Matthew 28:18-20).

Sometimes purpose looks bigger than you, oftentimes purpose is meant to scare you. If your purpose looks too big, it's because God is reminding you that you cannot do it alone.

After reading this chapter, has your answer to the question changed? ("What does purpose mean to you?")

_____

_____

_____

_____

Purpose Quiz!

What's the last thing God told you to do?

....that's your current purpose.

What is hindering your current life situation from becoming a vehicle to your next purpose?

-

-

-

-

If you don't know the last thing He told you to do, pray this prayer and wait for His direction.

Let us pray:

God, I don't know what my purpose is in this season. I don't know why I'm here (at this job, at this school, in this city, in this situation, with this person). I need your guidance. Your word says if I acknowledge you in all my ways you will direct my path (Proverbs 3:6). I need you to direct me, I need to know what you want me to do. I would hate for my disobedience to be a reason this season's purpose is repeated or unnecessarily prolonged, so prepare my heart and spirit for obedience if what you want me to do is out of my comfort zone. God, whatever it is, I give you my "yes," Your will be done in my life. If you have already told me what to do, bring it back to memory and help me to be obedient this time when you speak. Your word says in Philippians 2:13, "For God is working in you, giving you the desire and the power to do what pleases him." I pray this over me, and all connected to my purpose in Jesus' name. Lastly, God, I know that nothing is wasted in the Kingdom of God, so I thank you for the season I am currently in. Thank you for growing me in ways seen and unseen. Thank you for the closed doors and thank you for the opened doors. Forgive me if I ever thought you have left or forgotten about me. Thank you for being the one that knows my beginning, middle, and end. God, I vow; until you reveal my purpose for this season and even after you reveal my purpose for this season, I will continue to carry out my overarching purpose as a believer in your Kingdom—to Pray, Worship, and Serve the Kingdom of God. In Jesus' matchless name, Amen.

CHAPTER FOUR

Know Yourself, Know Your Worth

If the man or woman of your dreams walked up to you today, what is your game plan? Who will you say you are? Whose will you say you are? What do you like? What do you dislike? What's your season's purpose? What's your life's assignment?

Questions That Need Answers (QTNA):

→ What have you accepted in the past that you refuse to accept now?

→ What are your boundaries?

- → What are your non-negotiables?
- → What/who are you willing to compromise your relationship for?
- → What are your values?
- → What/Who do you value?
- → Are you willing to engage in premarital sex?
- → Are you prepared to explain your stance on abstinence?
- → If you are abstinent, are you prepared to resist sexual urges with or from this person? (Or are you only abstinent because you haven't had a date in a while?)
- → What's your love language?
- → What's your personality type?
- → What are your spiritual gifts?
- → Who do you say that you are?
- → Who would people say that you are?
- → More importantly, who does God say you are?
- → What traumas have you experienced that make you who you are? How are you growing from them?
- → How do you practice self-care?
- → How do you protect your peace?
- → Do you have a dating pattern?

You might be thinking, *'Why all the questions? I feel like I'm being interrogated.'* To that I say, if you don't know who you are, I mean who you really are, the enemy will tell you. In fact, he will show you, and the problem with that is, he's a liar. Whatever, whomever he says you are is not who you really are. When I say, "the enemy" I don't want you to think of some red devil with a pitchfork and horns. I want you to look at your dating history, your friendships, past and present, your family, or anyone. Ephesians 6:12 (NIV) says it like this, "For our struggle is not against flesh and blood, but against the rulers, against the authorities, against the powers of this dark world and against the spiritual forces of evil in the heavenly realms." You might have thought you were dating your long-time crush, but really it was the enemy using them to implode your life into destruction. The enemy is tricky; it won't be this huge situation where you'll be able to tell you are being manipulated. It will be slow, and it will happen in increments. Before you know it, you'll look up and the person you see in the mirror has changed. You ever wonder why, after you started dating *that* person you began to act like them? Or when you started hanging out with *that* friend you began to speak and think like them? That's why 1 John 4:1 says, "Beloved, do not believe every spirit, but test the spirits, whether they are of God, because many false prophets have gone out into the world" (NKJV). Every person that comes into your life wanting to occupy your time needs to be vetted, thoroughly. God can tell you much more about a person than a background check, but make no mistake, if you feel led to conduct a background check as if you were in the FBI, please do so as well. Lord knows I have done my fair share. The point is, you shouldn't be vetting your fruit at the grocery store more than you vet a person that could possibly turn your life upside down. A strong foundation in God will debunk any enemy that may try to come into your life, and into your heart.

Since God has created us; only He can give us our identity. You have to know and stand firm in the *fact* that you are royalty, you are chosen (1 Peter 2:9), you are a new creation (2 Corinthians 5:17), you are Christ-filled (Galatians 2:20), you are His workmanship (Ephesians 2:10), you are a friend of God (John 15:15), you are created in the image of God (Genesis 1:27), and you are a child of God (John 1:12). Never forget who you are. Walk boldly into who God has called you to be. Take the phrase, *What Would Jesus Do?* to the next level. Would Jesus allow someone to control His life? Would Jesus not test the spirits before entering into His presence and occupying His time? Would Jesus give pieces of Himself away to those who are undeserving, uncommitted, and not in covenant with Him? Would Jesus let the world give Him His identity? When enemies disguised as family, disguised as friends, disguised as a potential mate come into your life, the narrative must be changed. You cannot continue in these cycles of mistaken identity. If the enemy knows your downfall, he will send the same wolf, but in different disguises. The devil knows exactly how to make your knees buckle.

Think often on the verses mentioned previously and let God tell you who and whose you are. Let Him give you identity. Promise me, more importantly, promise yourself, before you announce another person into your life. Spend quality time with Holy Spirit. Take Holy Spirit out to eat. Go on walks with Him. Anything you can think of doing with a significant other or a friend, do it with Him. He's the only person that can hold a mirror to your face and show you who you really are. He will show you how your pride has ruined relationships. He will show you how your disobedience has caused you delay. He will show you, better than any experience ever could, how to be the person your future spouse deserves. Along with showing you, He will also anoint you to be with the one He has picked for you. He's the greatest life coach, personal trainer, mentor, and friend. Jesus is the standard on which all your relationships will flow. If you are not right with Him, no relationship will ever be successful.

The good news is that Jesus fits in every friend group. The caliber of all your relationships—platonic and romantic alike, will change once you have invited Jesus into your heart, *and* let Him be the leader of your life, i.e., submitted to Him. In knowing yourself, you will know your worth. When you know your worth, not even Satan himself can delay what God has planned for your life.

Boundaries (Non-Negotiables)

Boundaries are often the Cinderella aspect of relationships: overlooked and unwanted. When boundaries are neglected, it doesn't seem like a big deal in the beginning. Then one day you look up and the lines that should have been drawn to protect you are nowhere in sight. What's left is a broken person with more baggage and more pain than before. Morals compromised, trauma inflicted, and more accident-prone. Even though boundaries get a bad rap, they are a gift from God. The root of boundaries is love. Boundaries are proactive rather than reactive. Think about Adam and Eve in the Garden of Eden. God gave them free rein to everything that served a purpose or that could benefit them. Let's even look at a doubting Job who must shamefully listen as God reads His resume of work, careful to mention that it is *He*, who tells the sea to stop and go no further (Job 38:8-11). What if God hadn't set that boundary for the sea?

For those still not convinced, let's look at our Lord and savior, Jesus Christ. He was literally sent to this Earth to be our savior, so why is it that God, through Jesus' parents, prevented Him from going into ministry at 12 when Jesus desired? Boundaries. God foresees everything we cannot and seeks to protect like only a good father does. God sets boundaries with us, but when it comes to the people in our life, we fail to follow the blueprint of boundaries God has given us. It's time to change this narrative. Do the hard work today and create boundaries, your future self will be grateful!

What are the things you're not willing to bend on? No if's, ands, or buts.

Know Yourself, Know Your Worth

CHAPTER FIVE

Vision

What comes to your mind when you think of vision? What comes to my mind when I think of vision is Proverbs 29:18 (KJV), "Where there is no vision, the people perish: but he that keepeth the law, happy is he." The first part of this verse is so succinct, and oftentimes, overlooked. No vision= death. As harsh as that may sound, it is true. Where are you going in life? Are you just living day by day or do you have a vision? Your life and the life of the generations behind you literally depends on it. Take Joseph in Genesis chapters 37-50. He got a vision from God, and he ran with it.

God is funny though, He didn't show Joseph the part about being sold into slavery, jailed, accused of assault, and more in order for the vision to come to fruition. That's the thing about vision; it's not a step-by-step guide, it's an overarching finish line that you will one day see. Pastor Michael Todd of Transformation Church once said it like this in his book *Crazy Faith*, "God either shows us the destination without the directions or the directions without the destination" (Todd, 2021).[1] As frustrating as it may be, there is a reason the God we serve structures life this way.

Now, what comes to mind when you think of a vision statement? When I think of a vision statement I think of a business or a company. I want to change that; I challenge you to create your personal vision statement. I believe Habakkuk 2:2 (KJV) can explain the necessity of this. "And the LORD answered me, and said, write the vision, and make it plain upon tables, that he may run that readeth it." Before you get started on this vision statement, it's important to note that the vision is not man-made. Proverbs 19:21 (NIV) confirms that, "Many are the plans in a person's heart, but it is the Lord's purpose that prevails." You can have a vision of you winning the lottery six out of the seven days of the week, but if that's not God's plan for your life, nor a vision He has given you, God will not be responsible for its manifestation.

---

[1] Todd, M. (2021, September 21). *Crazy Faith: It's Only Crazy Until It Happens*. WaterBrook.

Acknowledge God in the process of obtaining a vision from Him and He will direct your path (Proverbs 3:5-6). Remember, when creating your vision, always think about how in and throughout your vision you will serve God, after all you are a servant to the Kingdom of God, *first*.

The purpose of this personal vision statement:

This vision statement is supposed to give you a baseline for your life. If someone wanted to know who you are, I mean who you really are. The person you are most proud of, but who sometimes misses the mark, this is the statement you could share with them. It's your elevator speech, if you will. When you write this statement you should also place a date on it. In a few weeks, months, or years, you can look back and see the growth you have made. That's why it's important to be honest with yourself when writing this statement. There is a difference between recording who you are vs. who you want to be. Don't get so carried away with who you want to be, that you neglect to record who you are at this very moment. If your future spouse were to come up to you right after you wrote this statement, they should be able to read it and know exactly who you are and where you are going. This statement should also provide some direction and clarity for your future when you get lost in the mundane of everyday life; or even when the light at the end of the tunnel looks further away. Let this statement serve as a reminder to put you back on track and inspire you to keep going. As you seek guidance from God in writing this vision statement, here are aspects of your life to consider:

- **Core Values:** What do you place high value in? What are your fundamental beliefs?

- **Essence:** Who are you at your soul level (mind, will and emotions), at your core? Without what or who would you cease to exist?

- **Areas of Focus:** What are the areas in your life that require the most attention and majority of your time? What are your priorities? Non-negotiables?

- **Skills:** What are some places in your life you could use improvement? How can you cultivate these areas in a way that will enhance your overall life experiences?

- **Strengths:** What comes naturally to you? What do you make look easy?

- **Profession:** What are some things you are striving or striding to complete or obtain as a professional? At what place in life once you've achieved it can you declare, "I made it!"?

- **Dreams:** What have you always wanted to do since you were a child or even since last week? Describe a life with no regrets? What does a dreamy life look like?

- ❖ **Passion:** What do you take pleasure in doing the most? What fulfills you? What would make your life incomplete?

- ❖ **Suppression:** What are some things that are hindering you from your future? What is holding you back from being the best version of yourself? (Maybe you want to add this to your vision statement in a solution-oriented way. Or maybe this is just something to think about).

- ❖ **Anchor Scripture(s)/Quote(s)/Motto(s):** What is an anchor scripture, quote, or motto that you live by? What is a scripture(s) that pairs nicely with your life? What word from God do you need to read that will ignite fire and strength inside you?

Now, it's time to create your own vision statement. Before you begin, say this prayer:

God, I ask you to come into my thoughts and give me perfect vision. I ask that you take my hand and help me write this vision with you. God, I pray that this vision will be used to propel my life forward. I pray that when I am surrounded by a cloud of darkness and I feel directionless, you will help me to remember this vision we have written together. Holy Spirit, remind me to look at this vision statement when I need strength to keep going, when I need light in a dark place, encouragement when I'm down, when I'm bored or when I

Vision

simply forget what You have said. God, I thank You that what You have spoken over my life shall come to pass. I thank You that anyone who comes into my life will be able to read my vision and run with it. I thank You that this vision statement will even inspire others to partner with You and write their own vision as well. Thank You, God, for going before me and preparing a place for my vision. Thank You for standing behind me to push me into vision. Thank You for walking alongside me as we see this vision through. Amen.

Create Your Vision Statement:

Date: _ _ _ _ _ _

Waiting Well

Vision

Waiting Well

Vision

Waiting Well

SECTION 4

THE JOURNEY OF MAXIMIZATION

CHAPTER SIX

A Spouse Cannot Be Earned.
They Are A Gift, Not A Reward.

I used to think if I was doing all the right things for the Kingdom of God, He would send the person who was to be my spouse when *I* wanted. I figured if I worked hard enough and prayed long enough, God would see that I *deserved* a mate. Almost willing to bet that God would take pity on me and conclude that since I was a "good" person I could merit a spouse. When the one who was to be my betrothed wouldn't show up, I would think it was because I wasn't as faithful to God. I even went as far to think it was because God didn't love me like he loved the others getting blessed with mates. I would see other people and assume that because they were seemingly living "in purpose" and had "made it" they had earned their spouse. I found myself paying attention to how they worshiped or ministered and electing to be more like them, concluding that their actions were obviously how they were blessed with a spouse. Thank God for revelation! Thank God for evolution in my thinking. Thank God that now I know the truth. You cannot earn your spouse and thinking you can is a dangerous place to be. You begin to equate the arrival of your future spouse to the number of hours you spend serving or to the amount of time spent praying. This type of thinking says there is no grace. It says that we EARN everything we have in life. This type of mindset thinks we can earn the promotion, the car, the kids, the peace, the love. It even says we can earn our mates. If we were children of any other god, I would agree, but the God of the universe doesn't work like that. The God of Abraham, Isaac, and Jacob doesn't bless people based on their own merit. I had to adjust my thinking, I had to come to realize that my future spouse would not be a reward, but a gift.

Thinking you can *earn* anything in the Kingdom of God gives off a James chapter two odor, minus the faith. It becomes all about the works, no faith. To clear any confusion before it cements, it's not either-or in the Kingdom of God; it is a balance. The scripture says, "Faith without works is dead" (James 2:14-26), meaning one cannot exist without the other. By all means, prepare or *work* for your spouse by walking with Christ, having dates with Jesus, reading your Bible consistently, serving, getting physically, mentally, and emotionally fit, going to therapy, etc. Simultaneously, you must have the faith to match your works. Here's something too often in the Kingdom of God we don't talk about or prepare singles for, brace yourself—doing all that work and having all that faith is still no guarantee for your future spouse's arrival. Especially when the root of these works become an idol-ish checklist for your future spouse's arrival. Submitting the checklist to God every few months and wondering if He has reconsidered. Understand that you can get all the therapy your childhood needs, fill your bank account to your heart's desire, go on all the dates with Jesus, but it is still not a key to the married life you desire.

As Christians, sometimes we get swept up in a whirlwind of fantasy, forgetting that Kingdom rules aren't the same as the world's rules. In the world, if we're doing what is asked of us, we get rewarded, e.g., a paycheck, a tip, a good evaluation, etc. In the Kingdom when we're doing what God has asked of us, we get called the, "obedient one". Make no mistake, God *does* honor our obedience, but not always with what we want, sometimes it's with what we need. The same thing happens with tithing. We are called to return the first 10% of our increase in the form of a tithe; this way God prevents it from being swallowed up by the devourer (Malachi 3:11). This is because it is our requirement in Christ. God doesn't have to reward us for this, but He chooses to. God baffles logical thinkers all the time with this concept. They think He operates in a formula, but that is a Prosperity Gospel teaching that has had its demonic blinders over the eyes and heart of so many for too long. Leading them to believe they can earn and even deserve whatever they are given. We must reverse our thinking; we don't deserve anything…in the eyes of God we deserve death, but Jesus so selflessly died for us (Romans 6:23) so we could live for Him.

You can work to be prepared for your future spouse, but God only knows when they will arrive. On that glorious day, at that glorious hour, in that glorious minute, that will be the point in your life's journey where it is no longer conducive for you to continue alone. When God presents to you the puzzle piece that is to be your spouse, it will be a season in your purpose that was destined to happen. It won't be because God wants to 'finally see you happy', God doesn't pair people together to make them happy. God is uniting Kingdom marriages because of the inevitable intertwining of their purposes that need to align in order to advance the

Kingdom of God—happiness is just a perk. When you marry, it won't be the time in which you can finally rest; if God graces you to marry, you will be married under God's authority for a purpose, for a mission, for intercession, and for a time such as this (Esther 4:14). Until then, if God gets more glory from you being single, you *will* remain single, but if He gets more Glory from you being in a relationship then you will be in a relationship.

I wouldn't be obedient to the Spirit if I didn't mention this side note—some people have been called by God (they know who they are) to a lifelong journey of singlehood. Not to be alone, lonely, or to live without a community, rather to be void of a romantic relationship (Study Paul's Journey).

There is no algorithm for marriage. That's why sometimes we might read about a person like Adam, already in his purpose, then a spouse is presented to him. On the other hand, we read about a person like Abraham. God presented Sarah, his wife, to him even before he got to the place of, "success." God presented these people with their spouses when He deemed the time was right and when He would get the most Glory, not because they cried themselves to sleep every night in loneliness. Good fathers will never give their children something before they're ready, especially something that could possibly destroy or hurt their children. When the time comes, your significant other will be a total gift from

God. There is nothing you can do to deserve that person, just like there is nothing you can do to deserve God's love and grace. God will never love you any more or any less than he does now at, THIS VERY MOMENT. You cannot do things to strengthen His love or destroy His love for you.

Re-read those last three sentences again.

Let that concept free you, it freed me. It let me know that I didn't have to be the, "look at me, God," type of Christian. God made me, meaning I cannot manipulate Him into my next blessing. It also means I have nothing to prove to God. I just have to keep being obedient, praying, worshiping, and serving the Kingdom of God. Trusting that one day, when the time is right, He will bless me with the one He has handpicked, the one He has handmade, just for me. The one whose healing has been placed within me and who holds my healing inside them. The one whose life trauma has led them to me, the one whose twist and turns of life have attracted them to my ministry. The one who will be an Earthly reflection of God's love, for me. That's who I'm waiting on, what about you?

As you meditate on these words and ask the Holy Spirit for guidance, remember this: Stop asking family members, friends, or even celebrities what they did to snag their spouse. God saw fit to bring them together because their union would somehow advance the Kingdom. God created their paths to one another via life's circumstances. What God has for them is for them. As beautiful as their love story may be to you, it isn't yours or your fate. You're putting these two people on a pedestal and applauding them for their extraordinary union of love. In reality, you should be putting God on the pedestal and praying that He extends the same unearned, unmerited, undeserving grace to you. Ask *Him* to prepare your heart. Asking other couples for their advice or even their prayers to find a mate is like asking a classmate for the test answers when the teacher is literally waiting to give you the answers. Don't ask someone who didn't create the test for the answers. Ask the one who knows your beginning, middle, and end; the one who has the blueprint to your thoughts, wills, and emotions. He knows who is best, what is best, and when is best.

CHAPTER SEVEN

Be Careful Not To Awaken Love Before It's Time

Song of Solomon Chapter 8:4

"Young Women of Jerusalem, I charge you: do not stir up or awaken love before it is time."

Since the day Holy Spirit allowed me to discover the verse above, it has always been black and white, straightforward, cut and dry. It has always meant, *wait*—wait for the appropriate time in which love will pursue you. Don't force a relationship in impatience, don't settle, don't grow weary in your waiting – just *wait*. That is until the scales of depth broke over my eyes and I was able to see this verse for so much more. God showed me a parallel between this scripture and what unfolds in Genesis 2:18, 20, 21, & 22 (HCSB).

> "Then the Lord God said, "It is not good for the man to be alone. I will make a helper as his complement.""
>
> **Genesis 2:18**

> "The man gave names to all the livestock, to the birds of the sky, and to every wild animal; but for the man no helper was found as his complement."
>
> **Genesis 2:20**

> "So the Lord God caused a deep sleep to come over the man, and he slept. God took one of his ribs and closed the flesh at that place."
>
> **Genesis 2:21**

> "Then the Lord God made the rib He had taken from the man into a woman and brought her to the man."
>
> **Genesis 2:22**

I want to stop here because here is the point of revelation.

In Genesis, God's word says, "God places Adam in a deep <u>sleep</u>." In the Song of Solomon, God's word speaks to the women of Jerusalem and says, "Do not stir or <u>awaken</u> love before it's time." Singles, God was so intentional about His directions for our season of singleness. It's worded so clearly in His Holy Book.

Man of God

Adam or *man*, if you are in a season of your life where, like Adam, God has given you clear boundaries of purpose for that season; and now you are ready for a person, understand that before your Eve can come, God has to make you over. God has been so gracious to allow us to read the most intimate moments He shared with Adam before He formed Eve. We see that before Eve was presented to Adam, he was working and communing with God. Then we see Adam was literally cut open and God took out of him that which could not accompany him into his next season. Ridding him of the thing that was no longer conducive to his growth. In Adam's case, he took out his rib, because with that rib Adam would have been hindered from his next blessing. Hindered from his next season of purpose, which was to be a husband.

It's Important to emphasize that before this season Adam was operating solely in *his* purpose. As Adam was being obedient, his season of purpose led him to the next season of purpose. A season where he could no longer move forward without a helper. Adam didn't arbitrarily conclude that he wanted a wife. At that point in his purpose, in his obedience, he *needed* a wife. It's also important to draw our attention to the fact that Adam was working all the things God *told* him to work. Man of God, the worst mistake you could make is to occupy your life, your season's purpose with busyness or work that is not a Heavenly mandate from God. You could be doing a million things society deems fitting for a suitable man, but if none of it is what God has told you to do, you are in disobedience and not in God's will. One minute spent out of the will of God is an eternity wasted.

I'm Just Dating Until I Find My Favor

I get it! Within the culture we dwell, it's customary to constantly look for companionship. When you're low and when you're high; society teaches us to have someone right by our side. But let's take the filter off and look at this culture for what it is—ugly. You've been tricked, bamboozled, hoodwinked, hornswoggled, and that's why you struggle to fully live in purpose like Adam. With this way of thinking you may never get to that place where you allow only God to take care of you and be the one by your side. Also, I hate to be the bearer of bad news, but you've been working overtime for no reason. Man of God, don't you know that you don't even have to look for your mate? God presented Eve to Adam. "God put the Man into a deep sleep. As he slept, he removed one of his ribs and replaced it with flesh. God then used the rib that he had taken from the Man to make Woman and *presented* her to the Man" Genesis 2:21-22 (MSG). God is willing to do all the work if you just commune with Him. God's Holy word does, in fact say, "He who finds a wife finds a good *thing*, and obtains favor from the Lord," Proverbs 18:22 (NKJV) but revelation from the Holy Spirit says that you don't know how to do it by yourself. God *presented* Eve to Adam. True wisdom knows that to "find" your "good thing," you must first find yourself. The best way to find yourself, is to find God, the one who has created you. Adam didn't get to the point of needing a helper by tirelessly swiping left and right and searching the streets for his favor. He spent time with God, which we all see is the best type of match-making preparation. When the time was right, God woke him up. Maybe your Eve is right in front of you, maybe you have known your Eve since you were a child, maybe your Eve *is* your next swipe right, or maybe your Eve will bump into you at the store. The point is, you will never know until God takes the blinders from your eyes and *presents* her to you, but the prerequisite to your favor is time spent in His presence.

What Season Are You In?

God is not monolithic, and trying to calculate the Father's steps is futile. Your story won't always look like Adam's: God creates boy. Boy communes with and serves God in his purpose. God sees it's not good for Boy to be alone. God presents Girl to Boy. Your story could be totally different. Nevertheless, use Adam's example and do the last thing God has called you to do. Allow Him to give you purpose while taking out what doesn't belong. Trust that He will only do this until it is time for Him to wake you up from your deep sleep, take the scales off your eyes and present to you the woman who is to be the bone of your bone and the flesh of your flesh (Genesis 2:23).

Woman of God

Eve or *woman*. Like Adam, you are also being made over by God. Unlike Adam, during this season you are being built by God. In fact, you are in total construction because God is forming and molding you to be a wife. I know what you're thinking. *I'm already formed because God has been preparing me to be a wife since I was a little girl.* To which I respond, He has; that, I cannot argue with. What I will offer for your consideration is that marriage is not the rose-colored glasses you wore as a little girl (not Kingdom marriage at least).

Woman of God, you are about to be considered someone's favor, someone's anointed. For this, you are going to want to be formed into the wife God needs you to be. Understand that Satan didn't bother Adam until he received his favor, Eve. Your presence is a mere threat to the devils in hell. At every turn the enemy will try to separate your man from you, his favor. In this season, oblige God. Give yourself freely over to Him and allow Him to place things in you that will prepare you for battle. Make Him your foundation and concede yourself to His will while He makes you in the image of His bride. This way, when you are presented to your Adam, the old will be washed away and you will be new. New construction is always more noticeable. Adam will be able to easily recognize that you are his good thing, his favor. That cannot happen unless God takes you through a season of construction.

What Happens If I Awaken Love Before Its Time?

Blood! Blood everywhere! From a hug to a handshake, blood is easily transferable, thus affecting all of those around. If you approach Adam in a season when he is on the ground, literally cut open by God, understand you will be bled on. This is why Song of Solomon 8:4 says, "Be careful to not awaken love." If you awaken Adam in the wrong season, he will be open, still on God's heavenly operating table, and he will bleed all over you. He won't have a chance to be the man that he is supposed to be. He won't be prepared for you, nor will he be prepared to be the husband he was created to be because he's not finished being the boy he is currently. This is why I believe people have failed relationships and inevitably turn their backs on love. Love didn't hurt you. Love never fails, love is patient and kind... (1 Corinthians 13:4-8). Wrong seasons hurt you. Bleeding Adams still on God's operating table who really never healed, hurt you. You never walking in your new construction or what you needed from God prior to, are the reasons you were hurt in relationships. Don't blame love for your erroneous missteps.

Let God Do His Thing and You Do Yours

It's important for us to understand that God's timing is perfect and to everything there is a season (Ecclesiastes 3:1-8). God has a way of telling you when it's the right time. We may not understand why we're still single or feeling trapped in a season, but trust that God is sovereign and sees the beginning to the end (Philippians 1:6). Let God do *His* job. While He's doing that, you should be doing yours. That could mean literally working a job to build wealth for God's Kingdom, seeing a therapist, indulging in self-care, getting closer with God, and serving the Kingdom of God with everything you have. It varies for us all. Find what works for you and stick to it until God calls you to something different. In addition, while being single, it is important to recognize the different stages of singleness—self-awareness is key. It is truly one of the greatest revelations God can provide a person in their singleness because it forces all blinders to dissipate. It encourages one to face who, what, and where they really are in life. With this knowledge recognizing the season you're in is so important because then you have a better idea of the direction you're going. So be sure to not awaken love before it's time, for we know that if you do, the consequences could be detrimental—not just to yourself, but to your future spouse and all who come into contact with you.

CHAPTER EIGHT

Why Sexual Purity?

Contrary to popular belief, purity does not *just* pertain to sexual purity. While the Bible speaks explicitly about remaining sexually pure—more than that God wants us to remain spiritually pure. He wants us to be pure of heart (Matthew 5:8). We should seek purity in every aspect of our lives. Purity simply means having no sin and being clean from impurities or evil. Our example is Jesus Christ. He is pure in all His ways (1 John 3:3 & 5). We must also understand it is a journey to purity. Purity equates to wholeness. Jesus

Christ is the only one that is whole, 100% pure, but as believers—through Holy Spirit, we have access to purity. Only by Holy Spirit can we embark on the journey of purity.

Now that we have a better understanding of purity in our everyday lives, let's get into sexual purity. This is what the Bible says about sexual purity—or the lack thereof.

> "Flee fornication. Every sin that a man doeth is without the body; but he that committeth fornication sinneth against his own body."
>
> **1 Corinthians 6:18 (KJV)**

> "It is God's will that you should be sanctified: that you should avoid sexual immorality; that each of you should learn to control your own body in a way that is holy and honorable, not in passionate lust like the pagans, who do not know God; and that in this matter no one should wrong or take advantage of a brother or sister."
>
> **1 Thessalonians 4:3-6 (NIV)**

> "Marriage should be honored by all, and the marriage bed kept pure, for God will judge the adulterer and all the sexually immoral."
>
> **Hebrews 13:4 (NIV)**

> "Now in response to the matters you wrote about: "It is good for a man not to have relations with a woman." But because sexual immorality is so common, each man should have his own wife, and each woman should have her own husband."
>
> **1 Corinthians 7:1-2 (HCSB)**

> "But I tell you that anyone who looks at a woman lustfully has already committed adultery with her in his heart."
>
> **Matthew 5:28 (NIV)**

Abstaining from sex until marriage and remaining free from all sexual immorality is what God desires for us. In a perfect world we would be free from sex outside of marriage. Free from perverted thoughts. Lustful ways and lustful images would be non-existent. This is what God desires for us, and this is what He had in mind when He created us. However, it would be injustice if I talked about the idealism of purity but neglected the reality we all seem to face. In the world we live in, to remain pure is difficult. We're exposed to evil, perverted things and images from the devil at early ages—sometimes born directly into it. In this world, if you aren't sexually active by a certain age something is wrong with you. If you have never seen pornography by a certain age, you're ridiculed. It almost seems like God asking us to be pure in this type of world is a setup. Don't look at me in that tone of voice. You know at least once or twice you've thought that living a pure life was a setup, as if God is trying to *make* you fail. Not to mention #purityculture you know the type of people that have every Bible verse to throw at you if or when you fall short of Jesus' example of purity but are not too far removed from their lust either. All to easily forgetting where they came from and judging you because you're still there. The pressure is enough to make you want to reject all things pure, but then I'm reminded of what was said in Ecclesiastes 7:20 (HCSB), "There is certainly no righteous man on the earth who does good and never sins," and Philippians 3:12 (NIV) "Not that I have already obtained all this, or have already arrived at my goal, but I press on to take hold of that for which Christ Jesus took hold of me." It reminds me that yes, God's people are imperfect, but God has factored in all our mishaps. He knew that we would use sex to try and find our identity. He knew that in the quest for love, society would pressure us to "prove" our love with sex. He knew that while the body He gave us would remain uncompromised, our heart and mind would be filled with corrupt images and thoughts of lust. He also knew that we would journey on the path of abstinence and fail more times than we would have liked. Through it all, He loves us the same. In fact, He planned on us tripping, but he also planned on us getting up (Proverbs 24:16). I believe that is the true victory; getting up and moving on, while healing from our past and not letting it define how we look at ourselves in the mirror. It is also forgiveness for the experiences that have unfortunately happened to us, as well as the mistakes we've made. It is not comparing ourselves to those whose route is different from ours. It's understanding that God meant every word when He said, "Therefore, if anyone is in Christ, the new creation has come: The old has gone, the new is here" 2 Corinthians 5:17 (NIV). Accept this fact, in Christ, we don't have to be perfect; Jesus is the only portion of perfection needed. I urge you, no, I beg you. Stop shaming and trying to suppress the natural God-given desires and hormones we experience. God knew what He was doing when He gave us those natural desires. He doesn't want us to suppress them; He wants us to present them to Him in transparency. It is impossible to turn off your desires until the wedding night. Be honest with God about your feelings because spoiler alert: He already knows. Have honest conversations with God as you walk about your purity. The war on lust is too big for you to walk alone, but with God, it is already defeated.

Marriage Won't Cure Lust

Lust is often defined as a burning passion for someone, while this is true, it is only half of the picture. The world will tell you it's okay to passionately burn for someone, especially your spouse, but it doesn't explain how damaging it can be.

Lust might start off with pure intentions, but it is stuffed with sin. Lust is the opposite of love. It's selfish, it's destructive, progressive, and addictive. Lust will stop at nothing to please itself. God created sex. God created sex with the intention of it being enjoyable for His children within the confines of a marriage bed; however, lust can be a reason why one partner is left feeling unsatisfied, sexually. Lust is in the business of self-gratification, constantly teaching its self-serving ways, programming you to only think of how you can satisfy yourself, completely forgoing 1 Corinthians 7:3-5. While on the contrary, love says a husband should take care of his wife and a wife should take care of her husband, meaning no one is left unsatisfied. If unchecked, lust will result in a futile search of desire from your spouse they can never attain. They will never be able to meet the expectations of lust, thus making you unhappy. This gives way to adultery, masturbation, and sexual perversion to only name a few by-products. Lust not only ushers in self-gratification, but also a false reality. The reason why the porn star you watch, or the toxic ex can give you the burning passion you're in search of, but not the person you promised to spend forever with is because it's not real. After a while, the porn star and toxic ex can't even quench your thirst, what's next? The possibilities are endless, and the road is not worth losing everything. "Then the lust, when it hath conceived, beareth sin: and the sin, when it is full grown, bringeth forth death" James 1:15 (ASV).

How Do I Practically Prevent Lust From Ruining My Life

You can't.

Fortunately for you and for me, there is a Man who knew we would fall into the cycles of lust. He knew one sin would lead to another, which would eventually lead to death and decided that He didn't want that fate for us. He died on the cross for *our lust*. He snatched the keys of death, hell, and the grave (Revelation 1:18) for our lust. Because of this, you don't have to be consumed with lust and neither do I. You don't have change in your own strength. God wants to carry this burden for you. While He is delivering you from lust, (because it *could* be a process) do and think on these things:

1. Repent- King David's lust caused him to commit adultery and murder, but he had a heart for God and a mind to repent. This is the prayer he prayed to God after the prophet Nathan visited him about his indiscretions with Bathsheba and her husband Uriah.

1" *Be gracious to me, God, according to Your faithful love; according to Your abundant compassion, blot out my rebellion.* **2** *Wash away my guilt and cleanse me from my sin.* **3** *For I am conscious of my rebellion, and my sin is always before me.* **4** *Against You —You alone —I have sinned and done this evil in*

Your sight. So You are right when You pass sentence; You are blameless when You judge. **5** Indeed, I was guilty when I was born; I was sinful when my mother conceived me. **6** Surely You desire integrity in the inner self, and You teach me wisdom deep within. **7** Purify me with hyssop, and I will be clean; wash me, and I will be whiter than snow. **8** Let me hear joy and gladness; let the bones You have crushed rejoice. **9** Turn Your face away from my sins and blot out all my guilt. **10** God, create a clean heart for me and renew a steadfast spirit within me. **11** Do not banish me from Your presence or take Your Holy Spirit from me. **12** Restore the joy of Your salvation to me, and give me a willing spirit. **13** Then I will teach the rebellious Your ways, and sinners will return to You. **14** Save me from the guilt of bloodshed, God, the God of my salvation, and my tongue will sing of Your righteousness. **15** Lord, open my lips, and my mouth will declare Your praise. **16** You do not want a sacrifice, or I would give it; You are not pleased with a burnt offering. **17** The sacrifice pleasing to God is a broken spirit. God, You will not despise a broken and humbled heart. **18** In Your good pleasure, cause Zion to prosper; build the walls of Jerusalem. **19** Then You will delight in righteous sacrifices, whole burnt offerings; then bulls will be offered on Your altar." Psalms 51:1-19 (HCSB)

In verse 7, David asks the Lord to purify him with Hyssop so that he may be clean. He asks God to wash him, so that he may be whiter than snow. On this journey to sexual purity remember that you might fail. You might give into sexual temptation—we are human. If you fail, don't run from God in shame and guilt. Run to the father, He will welcome you with grace and mercy.

2. Find out what's triggering your lust? Your desire to watch porn and/or masturbate. Ask God to reveal to you what is making you run to these things. (Comfort, peace, reassurance, brokenness, emotions, idol-worship, etc.).

3. Understand that lust is not a hormone imbalance or a medicinal fix, it is a heart issue and God wants to heal your heart from lust. He wants you to walk in freedom. Don't believe the lie of the enemy when he tells you that you'll never be healed.

4. Get into a fighting position of spiritual warfare. I don't mean legs shoulder-width apart in an athletic stance. In the world, that's how we fight our problems. In Christ, fighting spiritual warfare means having the faith to stay in God's presence and rest. Fighting in the spirit means sitting down to pray while the Lord conquers the enemy. Reminder: anxiety, frustration,

worrying, and fear come from not having faith God will deliver you. Don't let the fear of God not delivering you stop you from getting delivered.

5. Seek to understand not only the demons you are fighting, but the root of the demon's long-lasting impact of masturbation and/or pornography. Masturbation makes you a selfish partner and when uncovered can take you places you didn't intend to go. The world will argue masturbation is a release we all need, but just as Paul said in 1 Corinthians 6:12 (NIV) "I have the right to do anything," you say—but not everything is beneficial. "I have the right to do anything"—but I will not be *mastered* by anything." Besides making you a selfish sexual partner, what lustful thoughts are entering into your mind as you work towards your finish? They certainly cannot be thoughts about God the Father (Proverbs 23:7). Pornography gives you a false sense of sex and causes you to chase something that is not real or attainable.

6. Get an accountability partner and BE HONEST. Find someone in your church, at your job, school, or even a family member who is willing to hold you accountable when you slip and if you fall. Someone who won't judge you and will walk with you in patience and love.

7. Understand, that deliverance doesn't look like you never having a thought to go back to your past. Deliverance looks like you having the strength of God within you to resist the temptation from the devil when it appears. Deliverance must be sustained.

Questions That Need Answers:

Below are questions that will help facilitate thinking and help to construct some/additional ideology concerning your thoughts and beliefs of sexual purity. You'll also find anonymous answers from various believers and their views on sexual purity.

What is sexual purity? (Define it in your own words)

_____

_____

_____

_____

_____

"Free from lust and sexual sin."

-Anonymous

"Denying your flesh of sexual desires to honor God with your entire body."

-Anonymous

"Committing my body, my thoughts, my feelings totally to God. In other words, I am not my own, that, "I belong to God" mindset."

-Anonymous

"Sexual purity is the lifestyle of viewing sex, sexual activity, sexual body parts, and other people through the lens of God and His holy design and purpose."

-Anonymous

"Keeping your fleshly desires under submission to the will of God. Protecting your spirit from both the natural and spiritual consequences of premarital sex."

-Anonymous

"Being abstinent and loyal to your body. Keeping your thoughts and body pure."

-Anonymous

"Sexual purity to me is being led by the Holy Spirit in sensuality and sexuality. The church traditionally forces the congregation into an asexual box by ignoring topics

regarding sex. Then when a man and woman get married, they have a lot of sexual traumas stemming from being taught sex is "dirty" Through reading scripture I found that God doesn't ask us to suppress our sexual desires into oblivion—but to direct them to a release in marriage. And even better for our own safety. We can see the repercussions of disobedience to God's order shown in broken families, single parenthood, STDs/STIs and alike."

-Anonymous

When did the first signs of lust show up in your life?

"When I found porn on one of my older cousin's computers."

-Anonymous

"In elementary school."

-Anonymous

"When I wanted to masturbate after my second encounter with pornography."

-Anonymous

"When I was introduced to pornography at 12 and taken advantage of by a relative."

-Anonymous

"When movies started to show sex scenes."

-Anonymous

"When I was 8 or 9 I discovered pornography on my brother's laptop which caused questions. I didn't know what I was seeing, but I knew it was bad and I knew I liked it."

-Anonymous

"Lust first showed up when I had an encounter with my cousins, and we discovered it together."

-Anonymous

"Around the age of 12."

-Anonymous

"Lust showed up for me during middle and high school. I watched a lot of suggestive TV shows and movies which led to my mind wandering and wondering. My parents never gave me "the talk" so I created my own assumptions of sexuality. It was tainted by media influences."

-Anonymous

That you know of, in your family are you the only one who is choosing to remain abstinent? If yes, explain how that impacts your journey. If not, explain why not.

"Yes. Honestly, I've seen the toxic patterns from the generations before me and the ones playing out in my cousins/siblings. It reinforces, on a practical level, that I don't want that lifestyle. I will keep waiting. Even when it's not fun."

-Anonymous

"I am not the only one in my family. A far as I know it is only my cousin and I that have abstained from sex. My family has a history of children being born out of wedlock or premarital sex. My cousin and I both recognize this pattern as well as come to the revelation that the only practical way to not be a part of that cycle is to abstain from sex."

-Anonymous

"To my knowledge yes, and it's been a journey and challenge at times because it's like you're breaking this generational curse that's been so tied to your bloodline. But knowing that God has something great in store for your family because you chose to make that change is rewarding."

-Anonymous

"My cousin has informed me that she too waited for marriage. She was 27 when she got married. My other cousin just turned her life back to God and decided to wait."

-Anonymous

"My sister, right before she got married, went on this journey to abstinence."

-Anonymous

"No, I think it helps knowing that you're not in it alone. You have people you can discuss your issues and desires with, and they can give advice and encourage your journey."

-Anonymous

"I have never asked, but as far as I know, I am the only one who has remained abstinent. It makes me feel good about myself because I get to break that generational curse and tell my kids that it can be done."

-Anonymous

"My little sister. However, that didn't impact my journey. My journey was impacted by God. God and I had a plan for my journey."

-Anonymous

"Yes. I have seen support from my mom and confusion from my sister who doesn't understand in a deeper sense. There is a misconception that all men are disinterested in celibate women because "they'll get sex from somewhere"."

-Anonymous

Why did you choose to begin a journey of sexual purity and abstinence?

"I view my body as a temple that belongs to God and that his original design was for sex to be an intimate experience within marriage. My sexual purity is honoring God and only by his grace I have been able to abstain from premarital sex."

- Anonymous

"I believe this journey chose me. I was 12 when I went to a purity class and made the vow that "True Love Waits," and I was going to save myself for marriage. But they were really just words and for my parents' sake. A little bit before I turned 18, I told myself that I could pick. I could go all the way when I met the right person, or I could go half the way. Don't ask me what half means (lol). When I met my first boyfriend, the night I graduated high school and we began dating, something in me wouldn't let me go all the way. Every time I was to that point, I would stop myself and make an excuse to leave. Throughout college, before I got serious about this decision of purity, every time I would be close, I would stop. I always felt the Holy Spirit whispering my ear, past the other person who was whispering my ear (lol) to remember the promise I made myself when I was 12 and recommitted to when I was 18. They were just words back then, but those words stuck. Then I begin to intentionally not put myself in positions where I could slip up and from then on, I begin to live bold in my sexual purity."

-Anonymous

"I was taught from a young age that you are supposed to honor God with your body, and I wanted to do that. Not just because it's what I was taught, but because I am living to serve God. To live a life that is pleasing to Him for a lifetime is more important to me than to please a boy/man for one night."

-Anonymous

"It was by God's guidance and not my own merit or understanding."

-Anonymous

"I felt that my body was worth so much! I viewed my body as a temple and chose not to allow my body to be used."

-Anonymous

"While building a relationship with God not having sex gives me clear focus on things that matter outside of sex."

-Anonymous

"Wanted to do things God's way. Fear of God."

-Anonymous

"I want what GOD wants for me in my partner and I didn't want to be blinded by sex."

-Anonymous

What advice do you have for someone struggling to remain sexually pure?

"Well, first of all...yes, it's hard. Period. It is not easy to pursue purity. It's much easier to give in. So when you want to give in, ask yourself "Is this worth it?""

-Anonymous

"When I feel tempted, I take a moment to pause and let God know what I'm feeling/craving in that moment. Then I remind myself of 1 Corinthians 10:13. I say, "God I know that you have given me power over this temptation, over this desire. I know that you always give me a way out. Strengthen me in this moment to make the right choice." Then, I choose to do something GOOD. Go for a walk, read a book, watch a sermon, take a nap, paint, do a puzzle, blog, cook, clean, etc."

-Anonymous

"If you slip up...because let's be real: It happens. Please don't run from God! Instead, Run TOWARDS him. He is waiting with open arms to forgive you and strengthen you for the next time you are tempted."

-Anonymous

"I know it's tough. But this is what God calls us to do, I swear the delayed gratification of you waiting will be better than any couple minutes of pleasure. I believe it's a special kind of favor for the unions who wait."

-Anonymous

"Surround yourself with a like-minded community and remove anything that will distract or tempt you back to your old ways."

-Anonymous

"If you want to remain pure don't put yourself in situations where it leaves the possibility for something to happen. Also be careful about the things you're listening to, watching and sometimes the people you're hanging with because not everyone supports your lifestyle choices."

-Anonymous

"Pray. Pray every day, all day. Every time you feel tempted, PRAY. Every time you start questioning if you should just give it up and get it over with, PRAY. It definitely gets hard sometimes because we're all humans and we were made for a relationship, but God determines

when that relationship will come. Be patient. Your waiting won't be in vain."

-Anonymous

"I would suggest you find your "why". Find your purpose of being abstinent and allow it to be your focus."

-Anonymous

"Seek strength from God on your "why". The world is at conflict with the Word, and you'll see a lot of doubtful, fearful feedback from your acquaintances. Also, understand that lust is different from natural sexual desire. God gave us desire as humans to seek family and parenthood. Pray over every sexual feeling you encounter. What is the source of your feelings? There is also a difference between sexual suppression and abstinence. You don't have to hate your sexual desires or teach yourself that sex is "dirty" or "impure". Sex is reserved for marriage and within those confines you will experience no shame. Please allow God to teach you about your manhood or womanhood and be specific on who you allow to speak into your life."

-Anonymous

What triggers your lust? (Think deeper than... "Because I'm horny" is it sadness, loneliness, needing to feel something, etc.)

"The things I expose myself to or the things I give my attention to. It could be something I saw on TV or on social media. At other times it could be boredom."

-Anonymous

"Music (sexual) and "What I would do" conversations."

-Anonymous

"Lack of control in any area of my life."

-Anonymous

"I face lust most times in situations where I try to suppress negative feelings, specifically feelings of loneliness, unworthiness, or low self-esteem."

-Anonymous

"Sometimes the desire to be held or touched. Wanting to be wanted."

-Anonymous

"Wanting intimacy, physical touch and the sense of being in control."

-Anonymous

"The need for control in relationships with men triggers my lust."

-Anonymous

> *"My lust will surface if I'm manipulating a situation to favor my own selfish desires or viewing a man solely to service me. It's a game of playing men before they play me. When I came out of that life, I found out how much manipulation & lust tie into witchcraft. Natural sexual desires for men may arise if we are connecting through conversations, stimulating environments or mutual interests."*
>
> –Anonymous

If applicable, what makes you run to porn and/or masturbation?

"Boredom and hormones."

—Anonymous

"Masturbation/porn causes me to have some sense of pseudo control."

—Anonymous

"Sometimes when it is brought up, I ponder on the idea in my imagination as opposed to pushing it away or occupying my time with something else. Also, when I feel overwhelmed and desire to relieve those feelings (albeit temporarily). Also, sometimes when the idea of marital sex comes up but feels unattainable, I feel tempted to settle for lesser."

—Anonymous

"A quick thrill."

—Anonymous

"A need for sexual escape used to lead me to watch porn. I also enjoyed masturbating just because of the physical stress release of orgasms. It was an act of recentering via sex vs through building a relationship with God. The stress release was always temporary and never sustaining. My relationship with God now sustains me."

—Anonymous

What does the devil say to you when you are trying to resist the temptation of porn and/or masturbation?

"*"Just give in", "No one will ever want you", "Just a little peek won't hurt"."*

                                                             -Anonymous

""You might as well get it over with" or "You've done well. It's just this one time and then you can continue being "good""."

                                                             -Anonymous

"That I would never experience good sex, even in marriage and this is the best that I could get. Or that it will take away those negative/overwhelming feelings."

                                                             -Anonymous

"Other people do it."

                                                             -Anonymous

"It's a natural thing—everyone does it."

                                                             -Anonymous

"I still struggle with watching soft porn TV shows and movies. Sometimes the enemy will put suggestive videos into my YouTube recommendations when I'm trying harder to ignore them. It's a feeling of me "needing" to put those pictures in my mind to feed my sexuality. While I don't believe in completely cutting out suggestive TV shows/movies, I still actively try not to watch them all the time."

                                                             -Anonymous

If you have not started a journey to being abstinent, what is holding you back?

"Commitment issues."

> - Anonymous

"What if I fail?"

> - Anonymous

"I've never seen anyone take this journey; I don't want to be the first. Plus, I feel like I cannot do it alone."

> -Anonymous

"I have seen people have successful relationships and while still having sex before marriage."

> -Anonymous

"I'm sort of on the journey, sort of not. I fail every so often, but I know God acknowledges my willingness—hopefully."

> - Anonymous

SECTION 5

ARE YOU WILLING?

CHAPTER NINE

Are You Committed to The Pour?

Oftentimes, when I transfer a liquid from one bottle into another bottle, God reminds me of a prophetic revelation He gave me a few years back. He said, "Relationships are like the act of pouring. You have to commit to the pour. If you don't commit, and pour with little to no confidence, the liquid doesn't get transferred into the new bottle and runs down the side of the old bottle. But if you commit to the pour and start off bold, you will get a flow. Before you know it, nothing will be wasted. The old bottle will be empty, the new will be full, and your task will have been a success." Let me explain, there is an art to pouring or transferring liquids. Have you ever tried to pour a liquid into a bottle with a small opening and because you didn't pour correctly, that liquid ended up everywhere? That's because you didn't commit to the pour. You started off unsure and with hesitancy. Being unsure before a big pour is common, especially if what's in the container is valuable; however, that wasn't the fault. The fault was letting the fear of the pour or the fear of wasting the liquid stop you from pouring with confidence. You poured in a way that translated to *"Maybe if I pour slowly and tread lightly, I won't get disappointed or end up giving my all and it backfiring later."* Your uncertainty, your lack of confidence and lack of boldness in that pour produced a mess. Now, the liquid that was supposed to make it into a new bottle is on the counter, wasted. Wasted liquid isn't even the worst part. The worst part is towards the end, when so much has already been wasted, you finally get a flow. You finally get comfortable, but it's too late; so much has been lost. The pour is unsalvageable.

Okay, let me translate this back to relationships. At the start of a new relationship, you might be feeling unsure. Feeling like, "Maybe I should hold back." Feeling like, "Maybe I shouldn't give this person all of me or let them see the real me yet," in fear of being hurt. If I tread lightly or "pour slowly," I won't get hurt or disappointed, in the event that this person doesn't have good intentions for my heart. In the end, we see that this type of thinking leads to the type of actions that cause us to hold back in relationships and not commit ourselves to the process. Now instead, whatever that special liquid was that you took time to even attempt to transfer (your thoughtfulness, your honesty, your trust, your time, your attention, your heart) into the new bottle (your new relationship/new partner) is on the counter, wasted (failed relationship).

I know what you're thinking, *"Maybe I wouldn't have poured slowly if pouring fast in the past didn't bring about pain."* Let's explore that. Maybe it's not your fault. Maybe you did everything right and still got hurt? Last time, you poured with confidence and boldness and still got played. I hear you, I see you, I feel you, and I understand you, but I do want to bring to your attention a little thing called *over-pouring*. That's when you underestimate how much liquid is actually in the bottle and how fast it will come out. You pour with so much strength that the receiving bottle cannot take all the liquid and rejects it. Taking enough to lead you on but leaving the rest on the counter. Or maybe you saw someone else pour and the outcome was unfavorable, so you swore to never let that happen to you. Your second-hand fear is valid, but understand it is hindering you from moving forward.

It's time for you to stop holding back. It's time for you to pour with confidence again. New relationships can be scary, especially if you have been hurt in the past. A new relationship with old hurts, memories and pain will cause you to pour a little slower into the next relationship and give a little less of yourself because of fear. But examine the fruit of pouring a little slower? Where does the liquid end up when you pour slower? Yes, on the counter. I know that the last person took a piece of your heart when it ended, but why should this new person have to experience *only* the remnants of you? How is that fair to them and how does that provide a foundation for a successful relationship?

Am I saying go and give this guy/girl you *just* met your all? No, absolutely not. Pouring into a new bottle takes prior thought and prior knowledge. It takes discernment and prayer, possibly even fasting. If you have a habit of jumping into relationships because they *feel right*, you will often leave broken, bitter, outside the will of God and possibly even without purpose. If you're not submitting every relationship in your life for God to guide, what are you doing? Don't you understand the enemy HATES you? Does the Devil in a Blue Dress/Suit mean nothing to you? Please don't misunderstand, everything is either God arranged, or God allowed. The enemy has no power to take you out, but he does roam seeking whom he may devour (1 Peter 5:8). This person who has suddenly come into your life needs to be vetted. 1 John 4:1 says to test the spirits to see if they are from God. This person who you have fallen for could be the cause of your greatest downfall.

Many Christians get themselves into situations and ask God to intervene and take it away when the damage is already done. God is a protector, and He will save you from your enemies' snare, but when you are outside of His will, how can He protect you from the battle wounds? Even when God rescues you from the situation, there are wounds that the enemy will rejoice over because they will last even longer than your winner's title ever could. That's all the enemy needs. He doesn't need to win the battle, or the war for that matter; he just needs to wound you. The wounds keep you from purpose, they keep you from healthy relationships, from freedom, and eventually from pouring. Yes, you won the battle. Yes, you were delivered from the relationship. God will even deliver you from the next relationship, but are they worth the wounds?

    I have a proposal for you. Don't get excited, it's not that kind of proposal. What if you were proactive instead of reactive? What if you started off healed? What if on the front end you prayed, fasted, and sought God's face for clarity before moving forward in a new relationship? If this was the case, maybe you wouldn't have to worry over the sciences of a perfect pour. When God is consulted, when God is asked, when God is considered, He takes care of everything. He'll tell you when to pour, how much to pour, and when to stop pouring. He might even pour for you when you feel like you cannot. Not only will He do that, but He'll also heal the holes within the

Are You Committed to The Pour?

bottle you're pouring from. All you have to do is ask. Proverbs 3:6 (NKJV) says, "In all your ways acknowledge Him, And He will direct your paths." All you have to do is acknowledge Him in your attempts at love and He will lead you down the right path. Are you ready to commit to the pour? Are you ready to release what has been holding you back?

I believe we can often look back into our life's path to give us insight on the future.

Take a few minutes to write down some of the reasons you might enter a new relationship, uncommitted to the pour? Was it an ex, was it your up-bringing, was it you?

Say a prayer before and after writing this list

-

-

-

-

-

-

-

Now, I want you to make a checklist of what you need to do before moving into a new relationship.

Heal, if so, how? Forgive, if so who and how? Release, if so who and how? Consult God, if so, how do you plan to do this? Prayer, a fast, and a break with this new person to think clearly? *Deep breaths* (If they're the right person for you, they will give you time to hear and seek guidance from God. Love can be blinding, so time apart can bring clarity).

Say a prayer before and after writing this list

- ❏
- ❏
- ❏
- ❏
- ❏
- ❏
- ❏
- ❏
- ❏
- ❏

Are You Committed to The Pour?

❏

❏

❏

❏

CHAPTER TEN

Release It (Soul Detox)

A Time for Everything

There is a time for everything, and a season for every activity under the heavens: a time to be born and a time to die, a time to plant and a time to uproot, a time to kill and a time to heal, a time to tear down and a time to build, a time to weep and a time to laugh, a time to mourn and a time to dance, a time to scatter stones and a time to gather them, a time to embrace and a time to refrain from embracing, a time to search and a time to give up, a time to keep and a time to throw away, a time to tear and a time to mend, a time to be *silent and a time to speak, a time to love and a time to hate, a time for war and a time for peace.* Ecclesiastes 3:1-8 (NIV)

A Tie of the Soul

Soul ties are tricky. Soul ties will have you awake at 2am scrolling through their social media to find residue of another person in their life. Soul ties will also have you forgiving them for the 40-leventh time after they said they wouldn't do it again. Soul ties come in the disguise of passion, that's why they're so tricky. Maybe you're not familiar with the phrase, "soul ties," but if you have been in any relationship, I'm almost certain you're familiar with the feeling the phrase succeeds. It's that feeling as if you're literally stuck to that person. That overwhelming feeling when you think or see that person. The feeling you get as soon as a spiritual connection is made—that's a soul tie. Just to clarify, soul ties don't just develop for lovers. We can have non-sexual soul ties to friends and family members as well. For example, you and your best friend might share a soul tie. No, you all aren't sexually intimate, but as humans we were made to be spiritually connected; because of that, it manifests in all sorts of ways. God intended for us to have soul ties. He wanted us to be connected with each other, just as we are connected with Him. He envisioned soul ties between a man and a woman, under the covenant of marriage and He envisioned healthy, platonic soul ties among members of His body. Because we live in a fallen world, what God has envisioned is buried under sin.

Healthy Soul Ties

Healthy soul ties are a blessing to us all. Healthy soul ties are like a weighted helium balloon on a string. The string gives the balloon connection and keeps it from flying away, the balloon gives the string purpose, while God, the weight, the anchor, keeps them both grounded. Healthy soul ties improve the quality of life for both partners. They give more than they take, and they foster a healing environment.

Unhealthy Soul Ties

Unhealthy soul ties bring you to your lowest and keep you there. They stifle and destroy slowly, so it appears as if everything is all copacetic. Under sin and removed from God, we have unhealthy soul ties. In culture today, we call them "toxic relationships." Toxic relationships include, but are not limited to: conflicting principles, hostile communication, manipulation, judgment, jealousy, abuse, unsupportiveness, control, lack of security, conditional love and so much more. Toxic relationships could have started out healthy, but for a number of reasons turned toxic. Often than not, the signs have been there, but were blinded by lust, "love," titles, or even excuses.

Daddy and Mommy Issues

People underestimate Daddy and Mommy issues from being the source of failed relationships, but they are absolutely a reason relationships do not work out. Because your parents were your first example of love, the attachment or lack thereof from parents have a lasting impact on how your love is given and even received. Unresolved parental issues will not only be present throughout life, but they can manifest themselves in various ways in your romantic life. It's vital to come to terms with how you have been affected and be sure not to take that into your relationship. This man or woman is not your parent and they don't deserve trauma's residue that you have been avoiding for years because you thought it would *disappear*. In the same way, while the foundational healing is our job, oftentimes God will place within the person we are to be with the additional healing we need. That's why James said: "Therefore confess your sins to each other and pray for each other so that you may be healed. The prayer of a righteous person is powerful and effective" James 5:16 (NIV). Some things we cannot do on our own. Sometimes we need a partner to walk alongside us as we heal. What's important either way is self-awareness and for us to surrender whatever we are dealing with to God. Ask God to reveal your heart in the area of parental issues and/or childhood trauma.

How To Build Healthy Soul Ties

Healthy soul ties can be formed by ensuring God is at the center of every relationship you have. This is especially imperative in the early stages of the relationship. God should be acknowledged in all ways, and He should be the one casting, producing, and directing the relationship. If God is in place, you won't need to worry about constructing healthy soul ties—they will form naturally. Submit your relationship to God and a healthy soul tie will be inevitable. It's worth noting that yes, while healthy soul ties will ensue in an environment conducive to the work of God, it is an ongoing process. Even in the healthiest relationship, a left turn can be taken and ruin everything built. The enemy is cunning, sneaky, and always looking to catch you slipping. Always be on guard (1 Corinthians 16:13).

How To Break Unhealthy Soul Ties

In order to break unhealthy soul ties, like all problems (addictions or obsessions), they must first be acknowledged. Self-awareness is the best awareness a person could have. An unhealthy soul tie always affects and changes a person into something they weren't before. An indication you are in an unhealthy soul tie is if the person takes you further from God. He will never send you someone who takes you from Him, or someone who becomes an idol in your life. You are His child first and their significant other second. After self-awareness is gained, next a plan must be made to rid yourself of this person who is no longer conducive to your growth as a person, more importantly as a child of God. Once the plan is devised, execute it. Choose God–choose yourself and leave. Finally, be free and release all that has been holding you back, whether this is a literal, physical, or even prophetic release. Where the spirit of the Lord is, there is liberty (2 Corinthians 3:17), but in your freedom, be careful not to fall into a cycle; the enemy could show up the very next month within a different person, but with the same spirit you just left. Be vigilant and reflective on what it was that attracted you to that person and how you ended up so far gone. Reflect on generational curses that have plagued your family as it relates to the type of spouses chosen to build covenant with. The same spirit could show up in every generation to thwart God's purpose for your bloodline and in your life. Ex: every woman in your family has been in an abusive relationship. This is a curse that needs to be broken or it will not only continue with you but visit your children as well (Deuteronomy 5:9). This reflection could be one of the keys to prevent a cycle of unhealthy soul ties. It's also important to understand that breaking this soul tie won't mean an overnight transformation and that the desire you once had for this person has evaporated. It simply means that through God's strength, you are able to say that in spite of your emotions and even desires, you value yourself and God more than this person. You might even get to a place where you feel as if you cannot resist this person any longer, this is normal. Have an accountability partner(s) in place who you can be honest with in your time of desperation. Someone who can pray for you in the process of keeping this spiritual tie broken. It might even be years later and that ex you thought you were over, could walk into the same coffee shop as you and feelings of yesterday begin to flood your mind. Don't be so blinded by the good memories that you forget the toxic fumes you both created together. Forgetfulness is how cycles are created. Be on constant guard of the mind, heart, will, and emotions because your heart is most deceitful and will trick you into a false reality. "The heart is deceitful above all things, and desperately wicked: who can know it?" Jeremiah 17:9 (KJV).

It Is Time To Release It

Have you released your soul ties? I mean really released them or have you just deleted their phone number, blocked them on social media and moved away? If your life is filled with old, dormant things that no longer serve you, how can you make room for new things God wants to do for, in and through you? "Behold, I will do a new thing; now it shall spring forth; shall ye not know it? I will even make a way in the wilderness, and rivers in the desert" Isaiah 43:19 (KJV).

You have learned to live in the cycle of your dysfunction far too long. I know it's comfortable. I know you think there is nothing or no one else out there for you, but if you just give God the thing that you are killing yourself to hold onto, I promise He will replace it—with greater! Maybe it will be sudden (2 Chronicles 29:36), maybe it will take some time. Maybe He will replace it with a significant other who is to be your healing, or maybe it will be with peace you've searched for all your life. You need to release the old. Heal, forgive, and make room for the new. It. Is. Time.

As you identify what and who you are still holding onto, ask yourself these questions to facilitate your thinking. Once you find out what and who, ask yourself why?

- ❖ What are you holding onto?
- ❖ Who are you holding onto?
- ❖ Why are you still holding on?
- ❖ Who or what in your life is enabling you to hold onto these weights?
- ❖ What generational cycles and curses in your family have kept you unknowingly bound?

Understand that you cannot take your unchecked baggage to your next relationship. It's much too heavy for you, so it will be much too heavy for them as well. Give it to God. It is God's desire to see you release it, but it is *your* decision. What God has for you is greater than what you see now. The peace you'll gain from this RELEASE is greater than any relationship, job, bitterness (Hebrews 12:14-15), or unforgiveness (Mark 11:25).

Reflect on these verses as you work towards a release:

Philippians 4:8 (HCSB)- *"Finally brothers, whatever is true, whatever is honorable, whatever is just, whatever is pure, whatever is lovely, whatever is commendable—if there is any moral excellence and if there is any praise—dwell on these things."*

Philippians 3: 12-16 (MSG)- *"I'm not saying that I have this all together, that I have it made. But I am well on my way, reaching out for Christ, who has so wondrously reached out for me. Friends, don't get me wrong: By no means do I count myself an expert in all of this, but I've got my eye on the goal, where God is beckoning us onward—to Jesus. I'm off and running, and I'm not turning back. So let's keep focused on that goal, those of us who want everything God has for us."*

Romans 8:18 (ASV)- *"For I reckon that the sufferings of this present time are not worthy to be compared with the glory which shall be revealed in us."*

I Corinthians 2:9 (NKJV)- *"But as it is written: "Eye has not seen, nor ear heard, Nor have entered into the heart of man The things which God has prepared for those who love Him.""*

1 Peter 5:7 (NIV)- *"Cast all your anxiety on him because he cares for you."*

Prophetic Release:

A prophetic release is so important because it is calling what is unseen into action. Your faith, actions, and words are meeting and declaring a release into action. What is a way in which you could release what has been holding you back?

I used to have this small group in college called *Single & Saved*, my goal was to help singles navigate through their season of singleness, specifically as college students. For one of the meetings, I threw a release party. I had the attendees and group members write letters of what, who, and why they were releasing. From past hurts to soul ties, to people, to trauma, etc. I bought balloons filled with helium and instructed them to attach the letter to the bottom of the string and release it into the sky. At the time this was so freeing, as I watched the balloons disappear into the sky. For some, it was like watching a stronghold fly away. For some while their strongholds didn't disappear at that moment, it was the beginning of their release and for others, it was simply a prophetic action sown in faith.

As the years have grown, so has my knowledge of how balloon releases are extremely harmful to the environment. So, I strongly recommend you don't follow in my footsteps...

Below is a list of alternative options you can do as a prophetic release of any stronghold preventing you from moving forward:

- ❏ On a sheet of paper (the size depends on what you need released) draw a cross and write all the things you need released from you at the foot of the cross. *"Then great multitudes came to Him, having with them the lame, blind, mute, maimed, and many others; and they laid them down at Jesus' feet, and He healed them"* Matthew 15:30 (NKJV).

- ❏ Write down all the things, people, etc. you need released and rip it up. (Into however many pieces you need to feel a release).

- ❏ Garage Sale: Give away everything that is holding you to your past.

- ❏ Trash: Throw away everything reminding you or connecting you with your past (Be sure to take the trash out immediately after so you won't be tempted to renege).

- ❏ Redecorate.

- ❏ Block them on social media and delete all contact with them once and for all.

- ❏ If you never received closure, write them a letter. (Send it, destroy it, keep it, whatever you need to do in order to achieve a release).

- ❏ Create a vision board of your future without that person, thing, etc.

- ❏ Soul detox: This could entail a fast, abstinence, sabbatical, a book study, etc. Pray and ask God what a soul detox looks like for you. Also, reflect on this quote from the book Soul Care by Rob Reimer.
"...*People marry to the level of their brokenness. If on a scale of 1 to 10 you are a 5, the healthiest relationship you will have is a 5*" (Reimer, 2016). [2]

---

[2] Reimer, R. (2016, June 1). *Soul Care: 7 Transformational Principles for a Healthy Soul*. Carpenter's Son Publishing.

Bonus Release: Idol Worship

In the spirit of release. As you work to release soul ties, add idols to the checkout cart as well. Idol worship is so easy to fall into because idol worship is cunning. Chances are you're not building a golden calf, creating a literal altar, or chanting to some mysterious gods, but don't be fooled, while the Children of Israel created golden calves, yours might be something simpler or even more complex. An idol is anything that keeps you from being obedient to God. As a recovering idol-holic, I feel I'm not suitable to lead you in this release, but what I've learned is that God does not call the qualified, He qualifies the called (Romans 8:30). So, my suggestion is to do a study on the Children of Israel and how idol worship continuously had them in bondage. God will reveal to you how much He hates idol worship. As He reveals this, further ask Him to identify some of the idols in your life. When He reveals them, ask Him for the strength to renounce them and cancel their assignments over your life. Some idols might be generational, some might be seasonal, either way, they must go. (Idol References: Exodus 20:1-6, Psalm 115:4-8, Isaiah 46:5, 1 Corinthians 10:14, Isaiah 42:8, Psalm 96:5-6).

The time is now:

RELEASE.

SECTION 6

GET READY. GET SET. MAXIMIZE!

CHAPTER ELEVEN

Go Forth and Maximize

Now, all things discussed in previous chapters *must* be put in action, i.e. it's time to be about it. By actively working on these things, you are in fact, *Maximizing Your Singleness*. But before you start, I want to re-emphasize a few ideas and speak to the elephants in the room.

I've Already Maximized My Singleness and Now I'm Waiting On God

One never truly stops maximizing their singleness until the day of union with the one who is to be the bone of their bone and flesh of their flesh (Genesis 2:23). Instead of being imprisoned in your pride and acting like a Leviathan, Jr. (Job 41), have you ever considered that maybe God is waiting on you? Let me start over—whenever someone asks if you're seeing anyone, you respond with, "No, I'm just waiting on God." Well, have you ever considered that maybe God is waiting on you? Have you ever stopped to think or even ask God if He's waiting on you and if so, what it is that He's waiting on? I want to submit this idea to you for careful consideration. Maybe God is waiting on you to do all the things He's asked you to complete in your season of singleness. Then and only then will He send what you have been longing for. By not doing what God has asked, you are single-handedly holding up the process to the one whom your soul will love (Song of Solomon 3:4).

We must remember that God will *only* send a help meet, He will never send company. In the same breath, God will *never* send you to be company, only a help meet. Naturally, in order for you to have and be a help meet, you need to be working. What are you working on? Not necessarily in the literal sense of work, but what are you tending to that God has asked of you? What are you doing in your current season of purpose? Remember, Ruth didn't get recognized by Boaz until she began working in her purpose (Ruth Chapter 3). Eve wasn't presented to Adam until he got to the place of purpose where it was no longer *good* for him to continue alone (Genesis Chapter 2). Are you doing something that warrants help? Are you filling your time with company or being company? It's interesting how obedience unlocks new levels in our lives. Even the small suggestions God gives us in the spirit manifest into huge leaps in the natural. If God cannot trust you to be obedient to Him when it's just you, how can He trust you with someone else (Matthew 25:23)? Not just anyone, the one whom He has handcrafted for you. They are His child before they are your spouse and vice versa. Don't you know God would rather see you cry a thousand tears than to place you into the care of someone incapable of loving you properly?

When Will It Be My Turn?

I know right now it looks like God is preventing you, but really, He *is* preparing you (2 Peter 3:9). He is changing your perspective and will confine this season's doubt and what feels like a burden back into the crevices of hell. Ecclesiastes 3:1-8 tells us that God has a timeline for everything in your life and to everything there is a season and in due season you shall reap if you faint not (Galatians 6:9). Fainting looks different in many ways: fainting could mean compromising years' worth of sexual purity due to a lack of vision for the finish line. Fainting could be settling and calling that ex who will make an "okay" spouse.

Or fainting could also encompass you staging a coup in your life and seizing God's job. All of this seems tempting and with the enemy's help, can be decided within minutes. The children of Israel spent 40 years in a wilderness they were only supposed to experience for 11 days. What decisions made will turn your 11-day season into 40 years? As cliché and obvious as it may sound, the perfect remedy to this possible destruction is Jesus. At this place in your season, if you're not careful, the angst will be enough to take you out. There are a couple of things you must do: first, grab onto God (Genesis 32:26) and let Him be your anchor. When your emotions begin to drift you away and your thoughts are heavy with doubt, the strong anchor will be the thing that holds you still. Second, feed your faith. Faith comes by hearing and hearing by the word of God (Romans 10:17). What are you hearing? What are you consuming? They say you are what you eat: that applies spiritually as well (Matthew 4:4). You are what you consume. When you're running on empty and ready to give up, what is on the inside of you at your core that takes over when you have nothing left? Is it fear or is it faith you've stored up for such a time as this? Third, rest in God. It's so easy to want to actively fill your time with meaningless to-dos, but don't. Rest in God as a believer should. Rest in His presence, and rest in your battle stance—on your knees, rested in prayer. In this position "When will it be my turn?" will no longer be your question to God.

My prayer is that upon finishing this book and possibly even rereading this book, God will have downloaded supernatural specific instructions as you wait well throughout your singleness. It is not by coincidence that you have made it to the end, and for that, I know there is a blessing already assigned to you. I am personally excited for the change that will occur in your life because you have decided to maximize this journey from which all other journeys flow. Remember, it is not by might, nor by power, but by God's spirit (Zechariah 4:6) that you will find success, don't shoulder this alone. Invite into your process the Ancient of Days (Daniel 7:9), the one who has your hairs *numbered*, not counted, but numbered (Luke 12:7), the Wonderful Counselor (Isaiah 9:6), the Comforter/Advocate (John 14:16), and the author and finisher of *your* story (Hebrews 12:2).

I've included a place for you to sign and date. This marks the beginning of a partnership between you and God. By the mark of your signature and date, I am believing with *you*, that your season of singleness—your life, will never be the same, in Jesus' name, amen!

_____ _____

Signature   Date

SECTION 7

BONUS

CHAPTER 12:

I Didn't Maximize My Singleness and Now I'm In A Relationship

You got into the relationship because you said you were ready to love, so act like it. Do the work necessary to make your relationship successful. Examine whether or not you crawled military style through your singleness or walked with your head held high. It's no shame in wanting to be loved and wanting to be wanted, but do you have that kind of affection for yourself? How kind are you to the person you see in the mirror every day? You go to the doctor for every part of your bodily functions except your mental health. Why aren't you in therapy yet? Is it because you think you're perfect? Oh, I know—you think you can handle your deep-seated family and relational trauma on your own? No, I got—it's because you think this person will come in the form of a magic pill and be the answer to all your problems? No longer will you shed a tear because they're in your life. If you think this way, I commend your ability to dream up an alternate universe, but this couldn't be further from the truth. This person will only expose the areas you neglected in your singleness, as a child, as an adolescent, as a young adult, and as an adult. Don't get me wrong, at first, it'll be nice, it'll be everything you ever dreamed of. You'll look up and thank God for hearing your prayers, praying Philippians 1:3 (NIV) all day *'I thank my God every time I remember you'*. Then the arguments will ensue, slowly, but surely and the "thanks" to God will lessen and a Job 3:8 (NLT) prayer will be your new tune *'Let those who are experts at cursing—whose cursing could rouse Leviathan—curse that day'* (..y'all met). You'll think if only we could x and if y would happen then maybe...but if z, if z were to happen then it would be perfect, again. Neither x, y, nor z could stop the cracks in your relationship from spreading like the roads of neglected urban neighborhoods. No amount of alphabet soup could heal what you failed to let God heal in your singleness. Don't get me wrong—it's not *all* your fault. Maybe this person didn't prepare either—two peas in a pod, wouldn't you say? Nevertheless, breathe. The relationship is not next in line for doom; it and you just need some GTLC. God's tenderness, love, and care. The God-shaped hole of your life only has one remedy; in favor of you, that's God's specialty. Yes, I know you love God, God knows you love Him, but wholeness is the goal. This other person should not be your other half, you should already be whole. Two wholes coming together to make one whole; bone of your bone and flesh of your flesh (Genesis 2:23).

Go to counseling—individual and couples counseling. I know you just met and couples counseling seems premature, but we fight a real enemy who will stop at nothing to see your relationship fail before it even truly begins. In order to combat him you have to do things that seem unusual, things that go against culture. If therapy isn't your forte, seek spiritual healing and delve deeper into your relationship with God, practice mindfulness meditation, find a mental health technology app, journal, or find a peer support group and get into a bible based community. What's most important is that you do something to better yourself and your situation. Another important thing is understanding that you do not have to do anything alone. Invite God into everything you do, from therapy to meditation. Allow God to use these areas to work through you. Get His aerial perspective on the things that "make you who you are." Get your identity in God—that comes from sacrificing your time and spending time in His presence. As you do this, get into a small group with believers who have the same kingdom-minded goals you have. Where two or more are gathered, there I am in the midst is what the Bible says (Matthew 18:20). Gather and get your healing (James 5:16).

Growing Within Your Relationship

Your whole life you've liked only what your family, friends or current boo has liked and done what they did. Find out what *you* like, I mean unapologetically, find out the things you truly adore. The caveat is still managing to be in a healthy and growing relationship. In many cases, your newfound interest could be the very thing that drives a wedge between you and your partner. They might feel like you're changing and moving on without them. This is where communication and open-mindedness are vital. As you discover the new you, share that with the person you're in a relationship with so they can discover the new you as well. Allow them on your journey of growth and give them a front-row seat to the person you are becoming. While you're on the high of self-discovery, remember to give them time to process this new person you are becoming. They might have fallen in love with the person who doesn't have an opinion about where you all eat dinner, but this new person does; within reason, they'll need time to process the change. This fork in the road will reveal to you the character of the person you're with. If they are willing to accept the new you and grow with you in understanding and open mindedness, then they are the one for you and there is no room for the enemy to weasel his way into your relationship via this avenue. If this sounds like a full time job, it is. If this relationship is worth it, this will seem like your only option. This option combats the misconception that says you must exit a relationship in order to grow. When the real plight of love is personally growing within the relationship with the added nutrients of growing together. If you are blessed enough to have a mate that shares the same desires as you to grow, you have found yourself a partner that's willing to evolve with you in the relationship–hold onto that.

Of course, to break up is always the other option, and this would be understandable if your evolution becomes a threat to this person because they are unwilling to grow with you. To which you should thank them for their time and offer them a receipt. They were never meant to hold stock in your life for long–only a season. You might mourn their absence, but really you should rejoice. Some people love when your damage looks like theirs. You know the saying "misery loves company." Well, it's true, even in relationships. Through God, your self-actualization saved you from someone who would have tried to keep the both of you in a box your whole life. This break up will be unlike any other, because in this break up you have the answers you need and a clear path to your best self. Everything is either God arranged, or God allowed; He has given you a sign and a mandate to end it. Accept it in immediate obedience with no excuses. You might feel pain but embrace this time and stay the course of your evolution. If no one says it, you should be proud of yourself because I'm proud of you; more importantly, our Father in Heaven is Godly proud of you!

About The Author

Kayla Fointno is a three-time children's book author and a Special Education Teacher currently residing in Tulsa, Oklahoma. Prior to graduating from North Carolina A&T State University, she lived in South Korea for 8 years as an Army Brat! She is currently obtaining a graduate degree in Mental Health and School Counseling. Upon graduation, her hope is to provide and make accessible mental health services to all, no matter their socioeconomic status. When she's not writing children's books, teaching, or in class, she's reenacting some of her most favorite plays, screenplays and even writing some of her own. The process of film-making has always been a passion of hers and she hopes to one day produce, act, and direct. In the meantime, she finds joy in helping other authors throughout their journey of self-publishing.

You can find Kayla in any of these ways:

www.booksbykjf.com

Instagram:

@booksbykjf

@Kayla_jf

CPSIA information can be obtained
at www.ICGtesting.com
Printed in the USA
LVHW072030010323
740706LV00025B/2066